STARK

# ABITUR

Prüfungsaufgaben
mit Lösungen

# 2010

## Englisch

Leistungskurs
Gymnasium
Bayern
2003 – 2009

STARK

ISBN 978-3-89449-089-8


32. ergänzte Auflage
www.stark-verlag.de

# Inhalt



*Fortsetzung siehe nächste Seite*

**Abiturprüfung 2008**



**Abiturprüfung 2009**



Jeweils im Herbst erscheinen die neuen Ausgaben der Abiturprüfungsaufgaben mit Lösungen.

**Lösungen der Aufgaben:**

2003–2006: StD Dieter Hannack und StD Klaus Reitemeier
ab 2007: StD Dieter Hannack und StD Jürgen Naumann

# Hinweise

In Bayern werden die schriftlichen Abituraufgaben zentral vom Kultusministerium gestellt. Beim Leistungskurs Englisch stehen zwei Texte zur Auswahl (Aufgabe I: Sachtext/Aufgabe II: literarischer Text), von denen der Schüler einen auswählt.

Die Arbeitszeit beträgt im Leistungskurs 270 Minuten (einschließlich 30 Minuten Lesezeit).

Die maximale Zahl der Bewertungseinheiten (BE) pro Textaufgabe beträgt in der Regel für den Leistungskurs 200 BE. Je nach den spezifischen Eigenheiten des zugrunde liegenden Textes bieten sich unterschiedliche Gewichtungen der einzelnen Aufgabenteile an, die sich jedoch in folgendem Rahmen bewegen sollen:

| | |
|---|---|
| **Textverständnis und Textanalyse:** | 50 % |
| **textübergreifende Aufgabe(n):** | 25 % |
| **Version:** | 25 % |

Bei den Aufgaben zum **Textverständnis bzw. zur Textanalyse** ist die **inhaltliche Leistung** folgenden BE-Stufen zuzuordnen:

5 BE voll text- und sachbezogen; überzeugend dargestellt
4 BE im Wesentlichen text- und sachbezogen und folgerichtig dargestellt
3 BE einzelne Mängel in Text- und Sachbezug; z. T. Lücken in der Darstellung, aber noch klar [1]

---

2 BE gravierende Mängel in Text- und Sachbezug; Darstellung wiederholt nicht folgerichtig
1 BE Text- und Sachbezug kaum erkennbar; unübersichtliche Darstellung
0 BE völliges Missverstehen bzw. Themaverfehlung; wirre Darstellung

Für die **sprachliche Leistung** ergibt sich entsprechend folgender Zuordnungsvorschlag:

5 BE sprachlich und stilistisch überzeugend; eigenständige Formulierungen
4 BE sprachlich und stilistisch überwiegend korrekt; meist eigenständige Formulierungen
3 BE sprachliche und stilistische Mängel; z. T. längere Übernahmen aus der Textvorlage [1]

---

2 BE Teile der Aussage wegen gravierender Mängel schwer verständlich bzw. wenig eigenständige Formulierungen
1 BE wegen einer Vielzahl gravierender sprachlicher Mängel insgesamt kaum verständlich bzw. im Wesentlichen Übernahme der Textvorlage
0 BE insgesamt unverständlich bzw. keinerlei eigenständige Textproduktion

[1] Die Linie kennzeichnet die Schwelle zwischen noch ausreichenden und nicht mehr ausreichenden Leistungen.

Bei den **textübergreifenden Aufgaben** gilt zur Einstufung der **inhaltlichen Leistung** folgendes Schema:

4 BE differenzierte und sachbezogene Argumentation; überzeugende Darstellung

3 BE im Wesentlichen differenzierte und sachbezogene Argumentation; meist folgerichtige Darstellung

2 BE nur zum Teil differenzierte und sachfremde Argumentation; Darstellung teilweise nicht folgerichtig 1

---

1 BE mehrfache Abweichungen vom Thema; unübersichtliche Darstellung

0 BE Themaverfehlung; wirre Darstellung

Für die **sprachliche Leistung** wird folgender Zuordnungsvorschlag empfohlen:

6 BE sprachlich und stilistisch hervorragend; großer Abwechslungsreichtum in den Bereichen Wortschatz, grammatische Strukturen und sprachliche Textstrukturierung

5 BE sprachlich und stilistisch ansprechend; Bemühen um Abwechslungsreichtum in den Bereichen Wortschatz, grammatische Strukturen und sprachliche Textstrukturierung deutlich erkennbar

4 BE sprachlich und stilistisch nicht immer korrekt und treffsicher; Neigung zu einfacherem Wortschatz, einfacherem Ausdruck und einfacheren Strukturen; wenige textstrukturierende Elemente

3 BE sprachliche und stilistische Mängel; Verwendung von einfachem Wortschatz, einfachen Strukturen; kaum textstrukturierende Elemente 1

---

2 BE wegen gravierender Mängel Teile der Aussage schwer verständlich; deutlich begrenzter Wortschatz; einfachste syntaktische Mittel und Strukturen; keine textstrukturierenden Elemente

1 BE wegen einer Vielzahl gravierender Mängel insgesamt kaum verständlich; unzulängliche Verwendung von angemessenem Wortschatz und entsprechenden Strukturen

0 BE sprachlich völlig unbrauchbar und insgesamt unverständlich

Es gelten folgende **Sperrklauseln:**

1. Wird im Beurteilungsbereich *Sprache* bzw. *Inhalt* nur weniger als die Hälfte der maximal erreichbaren BE zuerkannt, so kann die Gesamtleistung bestenfalls mit „noch ausreichend" bewertet werden.
2. Entfallen auf den Bereich Sprache bzw. Inhalt 0 BE, so kann für den jeweils anderen Bereich nur weniger als die Hälfte der maximal erreichbaren BE vergeben werden.

Für die Bewertung der **Version** bei einer Maximalpunktzahl von 50 BE wird folgendes Beispiel gegeben:

| Fehlersprung | Note | BE-Spanne bei max. 50 BE |
|---|---|---|
| bis 3 F | 1 | 50–45 BE |
| bis 6 F | 2 | 44–39 BE |
| bis 9 F | 3 | 38–32 BE |
| bis 12 F | 4 | 31–25 BE |
| bis 15 F | 5 | 24–17 BE |
| ab 16 F | 6 | 16–0 BE |
| ab 22 F | 6 | 0 BE |

**Für die Ermittlung der Notenpunkte gilt:**

**Bei einer Gesamtpunktzahl von 200:**

| **Bewertungs-einheiten** | **Noten-stufen** | **Noten-punkte** |
|---|---|---|
| 0–66 | 6 | 0 |
| 67–77<br>78–88<br>89–99 | 5–<br>5<br>5+ | 1<br>2<br>3 |
| 100–105<br>106–112<br>113–119 | 4–<br>4<br>4+ | 4<br>5<br>6 |
| 120–125<br>126–132<br>133–139 | 3–<br>3<br>3+ | 7<br>8<br>9 |
| 140–149<br>150–159<br>160–169 | 2–<br>2<br>2+ | 10<br>11<br>12 |
| 170–179<br>180–189<br>190–200 | 1–<br>1<br>1+ | 13<br>14<br>15 |

Bei anderen Gesamtpunktzahlen muss das Schema entsprechend umgerechnet werden.

# Stichwortverzeichnis

## I. Points of Special Interest

## II. Literature



## III. Stylistic Devices and Composition

# Hinweise und Tipps

# Hinweise und Tipps zur Textbearbeitung

## Figures of Speech

### Glossary

In the 'Questions on the text' assignments you are sometimes asked to identify and analyse figures of speech (stylistic devices). These are expressions and phrases, which are different from normal usage or sentence construction. Their aim is to make language more beautiful and/or to achieve certain effects. As the texts used for the Abitur exams are rarely very poetical, nor the questions about figures of speech very numerous, we will not give you the complete list of these devices but concentrate on the usual ones and the ones that have already occurred in previous Abitur texts.

**Accumulation:** A string of similar expressions one after the other. When they increase in importance → climax, when they decrease → anticlimax
Example: He moved the whole company*, lock, stock, and barrel*, to Mexico. (Dictionary of Contemporary English, DCE)
Effect: Emphasis

**Alliteration:** Words beginning with the same sound
Example: Learn to say before you sing (Proverb)
Effect: Emphasis, force, rhythm of language

**Antithesis:** Showing the exact opposite in parallel words, phrases or grammatical structures
Example: Poor men seek meat for their stomach, rich men stomach for their meat. (Proverb)
Effect: Emphasis of content through contrast in form

**Climax:** A series of statements or ideas starting with the weakest and ending in the strongest
Example: Friends, Romans, *countrymen*! (Shakespeare, Julius Caesar)
Effect: Emphasis, surprise

**Anticlimax:** The opposite of climax: a sequence of expressions that decrease in importance or value
Example: For God, for country, and *for Yale.*
Effect: Humour, satirical

**Ellipsis:** One or more words necessary for the grammatical structure are left out on purpose
Example: In Essex he could go anywhere he pleased. Alone. (Instead of: He could go alone.) (L. L.Rice, Southern Exposure)
Effect: Showing emotion, emphasis

**Emphasis:** Stressing the importance of a statement, usually by using the "to do"-structure in positive sentences
Example: He does go to school …
(B. Vine, King Solomon's Carpet)
Effect: Of course: emphasis!

**Euphemism:** The use of more polite expressions for something the writer considers shocking or unpleasant
Example: rest room, for: toilet; to pass away, for: to die
Effect: The tone (or the writer) is shown as mild, inoffensive, or prudish

**Exaggeration:** (Also: overstatement, hyperbole): To make something greater or bigger than it really is (This is also a form of → irony). See also the opposite: → understatement
Example: They advertise in about a thousand magazines.
(Salinger, Catcher in the Rye)
Effect: Emphasis, humour

**Irony:** Expressing the opposite of one's real opinion. This only works if it is clear that the speaker doesn't mean what he says.
→ Sarcasm and cynicism (the bitterest) are stronger and more negative forms of irony.
Example: I was the goddam manager of the fencing team. Very big deal. (Salinger, Catcher in the Rye)
Effect: Humour, criticism, (shows the speaker's wit and superiority, underlines the real meaning.)

**Metaphor:** A poetical comparison that does not use the "like" or "as". It indicates resemblance but does not express it directly.
Example: All the world's a stage… (Not:… is *like* a stage)
(Shakespeare, As You Like It);
Life's but a walking shadow… (Shakespeare, Macbeth)
Effect: Poetical, vividness

**Paradox:** A statement that seems impossible at first glance as it contains two contradictory or strange assertions, but is intended to be true all the same
Example: Divorces are made in heaven.
(Wilde, The Importance of Being Earnest)
Fair is foul and foul is fair … (Shakespeare, Macbeth)
Effect: Surprise, amusement, makes the reader think

**Parallelism:** The use of corresponding grammatical forms and structures in a sequence
Example: What a day may bring, a day may take away. (Proverb)
Effect: Emphasis

**Personification:** Things, animals, or abstractions are given human qualities or are presented as persons (Can also be considered as a → metaphor – it compares indirectly)
Example: The day has eyes, the night has ears. (Proverb)
Effect: Poetical, vividness

| | |
|---|---|
| **Pun:** | A play on words: sometimes on different meanings of the same word (homonyms: the bear – to bear), sometimes on the same sound of two words (homophones: new – knew)<br>Example: Seven days without water makes one *weak.* (DCE) – homophone*: week*<br>Effect: Humour |
| **Repetition:** | Mentioning the same word or phrase several times<br>Example: Tomorrow and tomorrow and tomorrow… (Shakespeare, Macbeth)<br>Effect: Intensification, poetical |
| **Rhetorical question:** | A question where no answer is expected, as the answer is believed to be too obvious<br>Example: Who is here so base, that would be a bondman? (Shakespeare, Julius Caesar)<br>Effect: Emphasis; makes the listener feel he himself has found the answer and thus agree with the speaker. Often used in political speech |
| **Sarcasm:** | A form of → irony which is mocking, contemptuous, or aggressive<br>Example: Protesting can be fun – particularly if the weather is good. (The Guardian Weekly)<br>Effect: Shows the author's anger or contempt |
| **Simile:** | A poetical comparison using the words *like* or *as* (unlike the → metaphor)<br>Example: My love is like a red, red rose. (Robert Burns)<br>Effect: Poetical, graphic power |
| **Symbol:** | A word which represents or is associated with an idea, a sign of something<br>Example: *Dove* standing for *peace*, the *sword* representing *force*<br>Effect: Poetical |
| **Understatement:** | (Also: Litotes): Expressing oneself in a way to make something appear less important than it really is. Also a form of → irony, as it usually means the opposite<br>Example: The Queen was not amused. (She was very angry!)<br>Effect: Emphasis through apparent lack of emphasis |

## Practice

The following all examples contain figures of speech. Try and identify them. The solutions are given at the end.

1. You look as if your name was Ernest. You are the most earnest looking person I ever saw. (Wilde, The Importance of Being Earnest)
2. (A diary) is simply a very young girl's record of her own thoughts and impressions, and consequently meant for publication. (Wilde)
3. … the way you flirt with Gwendolyn is perfectly disgraceful. It is almost as bad as the way Gwendolyn flirts with you. (Wilde)
4. If I am occasionally a little over-dressed, I make up for it by being always immensely over-educated. (Wilde)

5. Your vanity is ridiculous, your conduct an outrage, and your presence in my garden utterly absurd. (Wilde)
6. … Edgar, who has seen me buy white paper about 36,987 times (Newsweek 2002)
7. I have dared to love you wildly, passionately, devotedly, hopelessly. (Wilde)
8. Today I broke off my engagement with Ernest … the weather still continues charming. (Wilde)
9. Oh, do let me read them, Cecily! (Wilde)
10. Did this in Caesar seem ambitious, … was this ambition? (Shakespeare, Julius Caesar)
11. There is tears for his love, joy for his fortune, honour for his valour, and death for his ambition. (Shakespeare)
12. … believe me for mine honour, and have respect to mine honour. (Shakespeare)
13. … the uncertain road he had yet to go (LK 89 – Martin Luther King)
14. … after the last glass of Pommard with blue cheese, it is not wise to rise too rapidly from the chair. That might be too strenuous. (Time, 1968)
15. (The House of Lords) has given the impression of being preserved somehow in aspic. (The Observer))
16. I think my father is like the Holy Trinity … (Frank McCourt, Angela's Ashes)
17. The stove showed what importance every one of us held in the classroom. (LK 96, adapted)
18. Familiarity breeds contempt. (Proverb)
19. Death pays all debts. (Proverb)
20. It is an outrage to bind a Roman citizen; it is a crime to scourge him; it is almost parricide to kill him, but to crucify him …? (Encarta)

## Solutions

1. Pun; 2. Paradox 3. Antithesis 4. Parallelism 5. Accumulation 6. Exaggeration 7. Accumulation 8. Anticlimax 9. Emphasis 10. Rhetorical question 11. Anticlimax 12. Repetition 13. Metaphor 14. Irony 15. Sarcasm 16. Simile 17. Symbol 18. Cynicism 19. Personification 20. Climax

## Tips for Composition

### 1. Comment

*Before you begin* it is recommendable to get into the topic by brainstorming, for example by drawing a mind map, starting with a key word and branching off further ideas in topical or logical order.
In the classic **argumentative type** you have to weigh some pros and cons. The structure is quite easy:

#### A. Introduction referring to the topic

Here are some ways of introducing your composition. Remember to keep it short though.

- a **quotation** (from an expert, a song-line, a proverb or other saying, what your parents always say, etc. They don't have to be literal quotes.)
- a **definition** of the key words in the question (e. g. What is society, what is misbehaviour?) It is recommendable to consult the dictionary, even when you don't want to define your key-words: you will understand exactly what they mean, you get paraphrases you can use later in the text, you find related words in the neighbourhood, you will see what the corresponding prepositions are.
- an **example** from your own experience or from a book or film, an article you read
- a **commonplace** like: The older generation always lament the decline of manners…
- a **personal experience** with the theme
- a **provocative question** or statement
- a **current** or **historical event**

#### B. Topic sentence introducing the pros (or cons)

1, 2, (3): Arguments, views and examples

#### C. Topic sentence introducing the cons (or pros)

1, 2, (3): Arguments, views and examples
You should first present the views you oppose (B) and then the arguments that support your own opinion.
For a greater variety in <u>enumerating and connecting sentences or arguments</u> you can use some of the following expressions:

- First(ly), second(ly), third(ly)
- First of all; in the first place, in the second place; on the one hand, on the other hand
- Moreover, besides, furthermore, in addition to that, similarly

To express <u>contrary or qualifying ideas</u> you can write:

- Although, however, yet, nevertheless, even so, whereas, contrary to

### D. Conclusion (your own position)

To round off your composition:
- In short, to sum up, in conclusion, all in all, as far as I am concerned, taking everything into consideration, personally, it seems to me
- return to the title
- show consequences
- present a view to the future

The **expository composition** is similar in introduction and conclusion, only in the main part one argument follows the other, with the strongest one put forward at the end. You should always and clearly stick to the basic structure of introduction, main part and conclusion, and use concrete examples to avoid being too theoretical.

Most students don't take the trouble to write rough drafts, to save time. This is quite o.k. but you should at least group your ideas in an outline, which you can stick to while you write.

When you are done read everything again carefully checking for mistakes in spelling, grammar and expression. Consult your dictionary as much as possible. Don't add new arguments.

## 2. Commenting on a cartoon

When asked to analyse a cartoon, you should first describe the scene, the persons, objects and the action portrayed in the picture. Then you should identify the title or/and caption of the cartoon and relate it to the picture.

As a next step you should recognise and decipher the symbols and icons used in the cartoon, e.g. a dove stands for peace, chains for bondage, scales for justice, etc.

Then you should be able to relate the cartoon to the political or social situation to which it refers and you must try and explain the message (what/who does the cartoonist want to criticise, which current problem does he refer to, who does he side with/ against, etc.). Finally you may say, from your own experience and with your own arguments, whether you agree or disagree with the cartoonist.

## 3. Letter-writing

### A. Personal letter (Letter to a friend)

| |
|---|
| Writer's address<br>Date |
| My dear/Dear/Dearest, |
| Capital letter …<br>…<br>… |
| Love, kind regards, best wishes,<br>First name<br>PS … |

Paragraphs
- Reason, thanks, excuse
- Subject
- Conclusion (wish, hope, looking forward to)

Colloquial but correct and good style

Examples: Defend or criticise the Bavarian school system (gk 1995 – II); Cathy's letter (gk 2006 – II)

## B. Letter to the editor

| Letter layout | Notes |
|---|---|
| Writer's address<br>Date<br><br>Name and address<br>of recipient:<br><br>The Editor<br>Newsweek Inc.<br>251 West 57th St<br>New York, NY 10019<br><br>Reference<br>Re: Your article on …<br><br>Dear Sir or Madam<br>…<br>Yours faithfully,<br><br>Writer's full name | Structure:<br>– Refer to the article/letter (opinion, appreciate, protest, suggest)<br>– State your concern, with arguments<br><br>Formal language<br><br>Polite and logical |

Examples: A letter about qualifications for a 'parenting licence' (LK 2004 II)

## C. Letter of complaint

| Letter layout | Notes |
|---|---|
| Writer's name, address, phone, fax, email<br>Date<br><br>Recipient's address<br><br>Reference (Re: …)<br><br>Dear Sir or Madam<br>– Your complaint<br>– Details<br>– Suggestions for settlement of the matter<br>– Express hope for favourable reply<br>– Set time limit, threaten further action<br><br>Yours sincerely,<br>(Or: Yours faithfully,)<br><br>Full name | formal language, polite but firm |

Example: Complain about a disastrous holiday (gk 2004 I)

### D. Letter of application

Form: see B and C

Structure:
- How you heard about the post
- Info about yourself (age, education, career)
- Why you are interested/qualified
- Readiness for interview, inclusion of C. V., certificates, testimonials, stamped addressed envelope

Tone:
Formal, enthusiastic
**Don't:** boast, flatter, make demands, complain about your present employer, let on how much you need the job

## 4. Speech

- Structure your arguments clearly
- Address and welcome the audience
- Use stylistic devices like
  - rhetorical questions
  - repetition
  - alliteration
  - metaphor
  - irony
- Integrate the audience (As responsible citizens, consumers, parents, etc, we …)
- End forcefully, with an appeal, a call for action

Examples: Write a speech for a meeting of property owners (LK 2003)
A speech at a school meeting (gk 2004)
A lawyer's final speech (LK 2007-1)

## 5. Interview or dialogue

- Don't just write what comes to your mind but structure your points in advance
- Introduce the situation or subject; save the stronger parts for the second half
- Conclude with thanks and good wishes
- Pay attention to the stylistic levels (formal, colloquial) of each partner

So far this type of task has only been tested in Leistungskurs exams.

Examples: A reporter talks to an athlete who has tested positive (LK 2004 I)
Interview an animal rights activist (LK 2003 I)
An interview with the Minister of Education (LK 2005)

## Tips for Questions on the Text

It is wise to answer them in the given order.

Begin by reading the first question carefully and find out **how many parts** it includes. Then go through the text with a **text marker** and highlight every passage that refers to the question.
Employ the same technique in the following questions with different markers. You may discover parts of the text which you have overlooked previously.
Now work on the questions by **using and connecting** the underlined quotes. Try to use your own words – the dictionary can help you to find suitable paraphrases. If you decide to use a passage make sure to **quote it properly**.
The following **question-types** have often been used:

- **How does the author arouse the reader's interest?**

  Hints for your answer:
  - headline, introduction, first paragraph
  - personal approach, personal experience, human interest
  - tone (humour, irony)
  - direct speech
  - examples, quotes, facts
  - surprise (unexpected turns, statements)
  - figures of speech (rhetorical questions, comparisons, metaphors, parallelisms, anti/climax
  - unusual structure

- **What is the function of the first paragraph?**

  Hints for your answer:
  - arouses the reader's interest
  - states important opinions, raises questions
  - introduces the issue

- **How does the author make his article appear objective?**

  Hints for your answer:
  - avoids personal opinion and judgement
  - states facts and figures
  - quotations
  - refers to scientific studies
  - uses controlled language

- **What is the author's tone?**

  Hints for your answer: Tone refers to the author's mood or attitude which can usually be described by the corresponding adjectives, e. g.
  - ironical
  - sarcastic
  - cynical
  - humorous
  - earnest, solemn
  - detached
  - angry
  - provocative.

  Another possibility is understatement or exaggeration
  Don't forget to corroborate with <u>evidence from the text</u>.

- **Characterize a person**

  Hints for your answer:
  - direct (explicit) characterisation: author, narrator, or persons tell the reader about somebody's character. Look for examples!
  - indirect (implicit) characterisation: the narrator gives clues from a person's actions, opinions, or choice of words what to think about him/her. Find these examples and draw your conclusions! *(s. Stichwortverzeichnis Gk III: Characterization)*

- **What kind of reader is the text intended for?**

  Hints for your answer:
  - The source: Time, Newsweek etc
  - The content: non-fictional reports, comments, descriptions, criticism, allusions to general knowledge
  - The structure: expository, argumentative, coherently organised
  - Style and language: figures of speech, expressions derived from Latin, formal (colloquial, slang?), educated words, objective (emotional?)
    complex sentence structure
    Usually the criteria above appeal to politically and culturally interested readers

- **Analyse the perspective/point of view**

  Hints for your answer:
  - **First-person-narrator:**
    He tells the story from his personal perspective and lets the reader share his ideas and feelings (strong identification). Problem: he may not be reliable.
  - **3rd-person-narrator:**
    He may be omniscient about all characters' thoughts and feelings, which leaves little room for the readers' own interpretation. His point-of-view may be limited, so he will tell what only he knows and feels. The reader will also identify with him, but not as strongly as with the first-person-narrator. The reader can only speculate on the motives of other characters.
    The observer-narrator strictly observes, like a camera, doesn't draw conclusions or speculate on feelings, so that his narration appears trustworthy and objective.
    Stream-of-consciousness-technique: The reader is allowed to read the character's unfiltered thoughts (which are neither organized, nor interpreted) and can make his own analysis.
    Interior monologue: Events and feelings are presented through the mind of one character, without interruption, as if he is speaking to himself. Usually the first person is used.
    Reported thought: It informs the reader, in a coherent way, without discourse markers like "he thought", about what the narrator thinks or feels.
    *(s. Stichwortverzeichnis Gk III: perspective; LK: point of view)*

- **Characterize the stylistic level**

Hints for your answer:
- choice of words (register): colloquial, formal, scientific
- tone: humor, irony, matter-of-fact
- sentence structure: simple, complex
- text type: expository, descriptive, argumentative, narrative

## Tips for Translation

Die Übersetzung nimmt in der bayerischen Abiturprüfung breiten Raum ein: mit 40 von 160 BE im Grundkurs macht sie sogar ein Viertel der Note aus. Das ist sicherlich Grund genug, sich eingehender mit ihr zu beschäftigen, zumal viele Schüler sie nur als lästiges Anhängsel betrachten. Die alte Frage, ob eine Übersetzung sinngemäß oder wörtlich sein soll, lässt sich sicher dahin beantworten, dass sie so wörtlich wie nötig, aber so frei wie möglich sein soll.

An dieser Stelle soll auf einige englische Konstruktionen eingegangen werden, die im Deutschen keine Entsprechung haben und daher vielen Schülern Schwierigkeiten bereiten bzw. Fehlerquellen darstellen.

Solche Konstruktionen sind zum Beispiel:

### I. Partizipialkonstruktionen

Häufig wird die Konstruktion in Schülararbeiten beibehalten, was zuweilen zu Unklarheiten oder sogar falschen Übersetzungen führt. Die wichtigsten Möglichkeiten, englische Partizipialkonstruktionen ins Deutsche zu übertragen, sind:
- Übersetzung mit Relativsatz,
- Übersetzung mit einem (temporalen oder kausalen) Nebensatz
- Übersetzung durch einen oder zwei Hauptsätze mit „und“ (Parataxe)

1. engl. Partizipialkonstruktion → dt. Relativsatz
   “A lack of mentors and role models, the working parent … all reflect the changing social and economic pressures affecting youth today.” (Gk 1999/II)
   „Ein Mangel an Ratgebern und Eltern … dies alles Vorbildern, berufstätige spiegelt die sich verändernden sozialen und wirtschaftlichen Zwänge wider, die sich auf die heutige Jugend auswirken.“

2. engl. Partizipialkonstruktion → dt. (temporaler, kausaler oder modaler) Nebensatz
   a) “Flung out of their native lands by war or persecution, … immigrants are crossing Europe’s borders in unprecedented numbers.“ (Gk 2002/II)
      „Da man sie aus durch Krieg oder Verfolgung … aus ihren Heimatländern wirft, überqueren Einwanderer die Grenzen Europas in noch nie dagewesener Zahl.“
   b) “… newcomers are still coming, close to four million in the last decade, not counting an unknown … number of illegal entrants.” (Gk 1999/I)
      „… immer neue Einwanderer kommen, nahezu vier Millionen im letzten Jahrzehnt, wobei man die unbekannte … Zahl von illegalen Einwanderern nicht mitrechnet.“

3. engl. Partizipialkonstruktion → dt. Hauptsatz mit „und“ (Parataxe)

   a) “… the traditional exchange of housework for economic support is becoming outmoded, shifting the foundations on which many marriages are based.” (Gk 1996/II)
   „… der traditionelle Tausch von Hausarbeit gegen wirtschaftlichen Unterhalt wird allmählich überholt und verändert die Grundlagen, auf denen viele Ehen beruhen.“

   b) “… America’s encounter with their land was … often violent, consuming much of the nation’s energies.” (Gk 1997/I)
   „… die Begegnung der Amerikaner mit ihrem Land war … oft gewaltsam und sie zehrte stark an den Kräften des Volkes.“

   c) “… crackdowns merely send refugees underground, forcing them to take ever deadlier risks to get in.” (Gk 2002/II)
   „… hartes Durchgreifen treibt die Flüchtlinge lediglich in den Untergrund und zwingt sie, immer lebensgefährlichere Risiken einzugehen.“

## II. Gerundkonstruktionen

Das Gerund ist – vereinfacht gesagt – ein Substantiv, das von einem Verb abgeleitet ist. Es wird gebildet aus dem Verb + ing. Es kann im Satz als Subjekt (z. B. Swimming is fun) als Objekt (I enjoy swimming) oder als adverbiale Bestimmung (Präposition + Gerund) verwendet werden. Als Übersetzungsmöglichkeiten bieten sich – je nach Gebrauch – die Substantivierung des Verbs oder Infinitivkonstruktionen an.

Sätze, bei denen das Gerund als adverbiale Bestimmung verwendet wird, lassen sich entweder mit einer Infinitivkonstruktion oder mit einem adverbialen Nebensatz (mit als; nachdem; indem; dadurch, dass …) ins Deutsche übertragen.

1. engl. Gerund → dt. Substantivierung
   Easing entry requirements makes good economic sense …” (Gk 2002/II)
   „Vom wirtschaftlichen Standpunkt aus ist eine Lockerung der Einwanderungsbestimmungen durchaus sinnvoll, …“

2. engl. Gerund → dt. Infinitivkonstruktion

   a) “… exercising control over who knows what about you has come to be seen as an essential feature …” (Gk 2002/I)
   „… Kontrolle auszuüben über das, was jemand über einen weiß, wird auch zunehmend als ein grundlegender Wesenszug … angesehen.“

   b) “… America is the only country where people are cajoled into buying food products because they are “sinfully delicious”.” (Gk 1998/I)
   „… Amerika ist das einzige Land, in dem die Leute beschwatzt werden, Nahrungsmittel zu kaufen, weil sie „sündhaft köstlich“ sind.“

3. engl. (Präposition +) Gerund → dt. Nebensatz

   a) “Vowing to act tough on illegal immigrants … plays well with the masses.” (Gk 2002/II)
   „Wenn man hoch und heilig versichert , hart gegen illegale Einwanderer … vorgehen zu wollen, kommt dies bei den Massen gut an.“

   b) “… it isn’t surprising that some of them give vent to their own fantasies by responding physically to the fictitious battle being played …” (Gk 1995/I)
   „… es ist nicht verwunderlich, dass einige von ihnen ihren eigenen Phantasien freien Lauf lassen, indem sie auf die Schlacht … körperlich reagieren.“

## III. Passivkonstruktionen

Das Passiv gehört zweifellos zu den gestärkten Kategorien in der englischen Sprache und wird sehr viel häufiger verwendet als im Deutschen. Daher kann man es oft nicht einfach durch ein deutsches Passiv wiedergeben, insbesondere wenn das Englische ein persönliches Passiv verwendet. (= **He** will be told later; **She** was being helped; etc.)

Als Alternative bietet sich an:

1. engl. Passiv → dt. unpersönl. Ausdruck (= man)
   a) "The emotional and educational impact on these children is just now beginning to be addressed ..." (Gk 1999/II)
   „Man beginnt eben erst damit, sich der Auswirkungen auf die Gefühlswelt und die Erziehung dieser Kinder anzunehmen ..."
   b) "Such factors are still assumed to play their part in producing crime." (Gk 1998/II)
   „Man nimmt immer noch an, dass diese Faktoren ihren Teil zur Entstehung von Kriminalität beitagen."
2. engl. Passiv → dt. Aktiv
   "Among headteachers the argument is often put that uniform reduces competitiveness between fashion-conscious people ..." (Gk 2001/II)
   „Schulleiter bringen oft das Argument vor, dass Uniformen den Konkurrenzgeist zwischen modebewussten Schülern abbauen ..."

## IV. Veränderung der Wortart

Manchmal ist es erforderlich, bei der Übertragung des Textes die Wortart zu verändern, entweder aus stilistischen Gründen oder weil das Deutsche keine direkten Entsprechungen kennt. Die häufigsten Beispiele hierfür sind:

1. engl. Nomen → dt. Verb oder Adjektiv
   Hierher gehören Ausdrücke wie "to make a complete mess of sth" (etwas total durcheinander bringen); "to have difficulty in doing sth." (sich schwer tun mit etwas), "some sort of material" (ein bestimmtes Material) oder "in effect" (tatsächlich).
   a) "Most people have long accepted the need to provide some information about themselves ..." (Gk 2002/I)
   „Die meisten Leute haben sich längst damit abgefunden, dass sie ein bisschen Information über sich geben müssen ..."
   b) "Easing entry requirements makes good economic sense ..." (Gk 2002/II)
   „Vom wirtschaftlichen Standpunkt aus ist eine Lockerung der Einwanderungsbestimmungen durchaus sinnvoll ..."
   c) "... it is possible to discern among the young an insensitivity to nuances of language." (Gk 1995/II)
   „... man kann bei Jugendlichen feststellen, dass sie unempfindlich sind für feine Unterschiede in der Sprache."
2. engl. Verb → dt. Adverb
   Das Englische bezeichnet die Art und Weise eines Geschehens häufig durch verbale Fügungen, denen im Deutschen Adverbien entsprechen, z. B.: "to be likely to do sth." (wahrscheinlich etw. tun), "to happen to do sth." (zufällig etw. tun), "to keep doing sth." (weitermachen) und "to be sure to do sth." (sicherlich etw. tun).

a) "Successive generations are likely to be more thoroughly assimilated ..." (Gk 1996/1)
„Nachfolgende Generationen sind wahrscheinlich besser angepasst ..."

b) "... the region not only did not falter economically, but continued right on with an industrial expansion ..." (Gk 1997/II)
„... die Gegend wurde nicht nur nicht wirtschaftlich schwächer, sondern erlebte auch weiterhin einen industriellen Aufschwung ..."

c) "... exercising control over who knows what about you has ... come to be seen as an essential feature of a civilised society." (Gk 2002/I)
„... Kontrolle auszuüben über das, was jemand über einen weiß, wird ... zunehmend als ein grundlegender Wesenszug einer zivilisierten Gesellschaft angesehen."

## V. Fremdwörter

Ein heftig umstrittenes Thema bei Übersetzungen ist, in wie weit man Fremdwörter stehen lassen darf, bzw. wann man sie durch ein deutsches Wort ersetzen muss. Völlige Einigkeit wird man hier nicht erzielen, aber als Faustregel gilt, dass allgemein gebräuchliche Fremdwörter and Fachbegriffe (wie z. B. Computer, Horizont, Alternative, Demokratie usw.) verwendet werden dürfen, dass man das Fremdwort jedoch immer dann, wenn es ein gutes deutsches Wort dafür gibt, ersetzen sollte (career = Berufsweg, Laufbahn; creatures = Geschöpfe; consumption = Verbrauch).

Gelegentlich kann es auch notwendig sein, ein Fremdwort durch ein anderes zu ersetzen, wenn das ursprüngliche z. B. als zu stark oder zu schwach erscheint.

Beispiele:

1. Ersatz der Fremdwörter notwendig
   a) "... the emotional and educational impact ..." (Gk 1999/II)
   „... die Auswirkungen auf die Gefühlswelt und die Erziehung ..."
   b) "According to experts on adolescent development, children now spend significantly less time in the company of adults than they did a few decades ago." (Gk 1999/II)
   „Nach Aussagen von Fachleuten für die Entwicklung von Jugendlichen verbringen Kinder jetzt bedeutend weniger Zeit in der Gesellschaft von Erwachsenen als dies vor einigen Jahrzehnten der Fall war."

2. Fremdwörter werden beibehalten
   a) "New information technology offers huge benefits ..." (Gk 2002/I)
   „Die neue Informationstechnologie bietet riesige Vorteile ..."
   b) "Such factors are still assumed to play their part in producing crime." (Gk 1998/II)
   „Man nimmt immer noch an, dass diese Faktoren ihren Teil zur Entstehung von Kriminalität beitagen."
   c) "No issue generates more emotion ... Vowing to be tough on illegal immigrants ... (Gk 2002/II)
   „Kein Problem weckt mehr Emotionen ... Wenn man hoch und heilig verspricht, hart gegen illegale Einwanderer vorzugehen ..."

3. Ersatz eines Fremdwortes durch ein anderes
   "Britain pulled back from total abolition." (Gk 2001/II)
   „Großbritannien zog sich von der kompletten Abschaffung wieder zurück."

## Tips for the Exam

- Good preparation makes for a clear conscience, less excitement and fewer mistakes!

- **Select** the task according to the following criteria:
  Interest in the topic
  Comprehension of the text and the assignments
  Difficulty of the translation (50 BE!)
  Attractiveness of a composition topic (50 BE!)

- Make a **timetable** for the three parts and check during the exam whether you abide by it. It is better to drop a task for the time being than to get stuck with it. Return to it after you have finished the rest. Reserve some time at the end to go over your work again carefully.

- Be sure to understand exactly what the **questions** require you to answer. Sometimes there are double or triple aspects in one question. Highlight the passages in the text with different markers for the different questions before you answer them in your own words. You may quote – but not excessively.

- Please don't forget a question! This always happens to some students. It really is advisable to answer the questions in the given order.

- Before you write your **composition** read the topical question carefully, outline your ideas and arguments on a separate piece of paper. Make sure you consider a proper introduction and conclusion.

- **Use the whole time** that is at your disposal. Before you hand your exam in make sure to **check** the following points:

| | |
|---|---|
| Questions: | Do my answers really and completely correspond to the questions? |
| Composition: | Does the content cover the topic? |
| Translation: | Have I overlooked any words? Are the tenses translated correctly? |
| Whole text: | Tenses? Prepositions? Expressions? |
| If you have time: | Look up words you are not confident with in your dictionary. |

# Prüfungsaufgaben

**Leistungskurs Englisch 2003**
**Textaufgabe I**

## Plato, Parliament and the British fox

"When names, definitions, sights and other sense-impressions are rubbed together and tested amicably by men employing question and answer with no malicious rivalry, suddenly there shines forth understanding." Britain's debate on foxhunting has fallen short of this Platonic[1] ideal. The debate has been more malicious than amicable; and at the end of it neither side appears to understand the other better than it did at the beginning. All the same, contrary to the defeated yelps of some of hunting's shriller advocates, there was nothing undemocratic about the House of Commons' vote to ban hunting with dogs. In a way, the decision was four times more democratic than usual.

First, the Labour Party could not have made its intentions any plainer than it did in the manifesto on which it was elected in1997, which said that the party strongly opposed "the so-called sport" of hunting with hounds and intended to let MPs vote on whether to ban it. Second, if the arguments on both sides have not been tested as amicably as Plato might have wished, they have at least been tested thoroughly. Hunting's supporters and opponents have marshalled the expert opinions and lurid photographs convenient to their respective arguments, and plastered them over newspapers and billboards. Jack Straw[2] went to the trouble of asking for an impartial investigation of the facts from Lord Burns[3], who cogitated mightily and reached the memorable conclusion that the killing of a fox by hounds "seriously compromises the welfare of the fox". Third, when at last the Commons voted this week, the vote was "free", as the government had promised it would be. MPs were allowed to vote in accordance with their individual consciences (or at least their individual calculations) instead of having to stick to their parties' lines. Fourth, MPs were not presented with a simple yes or no alternative, as they usually are. They could vote either for a total ban, or for regulation of the sport, or for self-regulation, or against all of the above. Mr Straw himself voted to regulate hunting, not to prohibit it. His Tory shadow, Ann Widdecombe, consulted a furry corner of her steely heart and favoured a ban.

In short, far from being undemocratic, this week saw a perfect demonstration of democracy. That is the whole trouble. The vote demonstrated perfectly that unless political leaders are careful, democracy seriously compromises the liberty of minorities.

Some of the people who feel passionately about the welfare of the fox simply refuse to acknowledge that to ban foxhunting is to curtail a liberty. But liberty is the pre-eminent issue. Although only a minority of people hunt with dogs in Britain, it is a sizeable minority as well as a vocal one. Of nearly a quarter of a million people who hunt four-legged creatures, some 180,000 are involved in hunting foxes and deer. Of these, many care a good deal about what the Labour Party dismisses as their "so-called sport". Needless to say, the defenders of hunting exaggerate the impact that a ban would have on rural jobs and the rural way of life. But exaggeration is not the same thing as invention. Lord Burns concluded in his report that thousands of people would lose their jobs if hunting were banned. He accepted that in some areas hunting might still be the best way of keeping the fox population under control. He also found that in some communities hunting remained a "significant" cohesive force. Whatever city types think, foxhunting is not just the sadistic pastime of the rich. It is an ancient sport that matters to many people. If politicians make it illegal, they need a good reason.

To most MPs, the reason is self-evident: foxhunting, they say, is cruel. Previous governments have legislated to prevent cruelty to animals. Having banned bear-baiting, why not foxhunting?

It is a reasonable question. The answer, unless you are an animal-rights fundamentalist, is that the line must be drawn somewhere. Otherwise, the logical sequel to a ban on foxhunting is a ban on all shooting, fishing, the use of animals in experiments, and the rearing for slaughter of poultry and cattle. Politicians are entitled to move the existing line, but ought at least to aim for some proportionality. In other words, the welfare benefit they confer on the animal ought to be commensurate with the cost they impose on liberty. In this case, it is not. The plain fact is that not even Parliament can make the lot of the fox a happy one. Of the 400,000 or so foxes that die every year, few expire peacefully in bed. About 100,000 are squashed by cars, 80,000 are shot and 30,000 are snared. Only 22,000 are killed in hunts. And Lord Burns gave warning that although hunting with hounds compromised the welfare of the fox, a ban might compromise it further by causing more of them to be killed by shotguns and snares.

What next? The elected majority must have its way. Tony Blair has already said as much to the House of Lords, where the battle now moves. Some defenders of hunting – and some who oppose hunting but defend liberty – hope voters will punish Mr Blair for engineering this outcome. That is wishful thinking. Polls suggest that a ban could be popular. It will have been arrived at by impeccable democratic methods. It just happens to be wrong.

From: *The Economist*, 18 January 2001

1 Platonic (adj.): *here:* referring to the philosopher Plato
2 Jack Straw: British Home Secretary
3 Lord Burns: an eminent former civil servant

**Worksheet:**

maximum number of points attainable

**I. Questions on the text**

Read all the questions first, then answer them in the given order. Use your own words as far as is appropriate.

1. "In a way, the decision was four times more democratic than usual." (l. 8). With what arguments does the writer back up his statement? — 20
2. Explain why the writer does not agree with the parliamentary decision to ban foxhunting. Summarize the reasons he gives in lines 27–43. — 20
3. How does the writer deal with the argument that foxhunting should be banned because it is cruel? Outline his train of thought. — 20
4. Examine the function of the third paragraph. How does the writer achieve the intended effect? — 10
5. What aspects hinted at in the text substantiate and illustrate the writer's contention that "Britain's debate on foxhunting has fallen short" (l. 3) of the Platonic ideal of a strictly rational and fair debate? — 10
6. Show how the writer uses tone and language to convey to the reader that he takes some of the issues raised more seriously than others. — 20

## II. Composition

Choose *one* of the following topics. Write about 250 to 300 words. 50

1. "Democracy is the worst form of government except all those other forms that have been tried from time to time." (Winston Churchill). Do you agree with this statement?
2. "The credibility of any political system depends on how it deals with minorities." Discuss.
3. Is the liberty of the hunter a higher value than the right to life of the hunted?
4. At a fashion show an animal-rights activist has thrown bags of paint at a model presenting a fur coat.
   You have interviewed this activist. Write up the interview for publication in your magazine.

## III. Translation

Translate the following text into German: 50

200

Many Britons wonder what all the fuss is about. Why – with a disintegrating public-transport system, overburdened hospitals, failing schools and a country-side devastated by the ravages of foot-and-mouth disease – is foxhunting the one issue that really excites parliamentary passions?

Could the real motive behind banning the sport be spite, a way of getting at those toffs[1] on horseback, a last gasp of the class war? (And even this sentiment is misplaced, since half the hunt might be shopkeepers and small farmers.) Yves Lecoq[2] believes so, and says that a ban will convince many Europeans that "British society still hasn't overcome the class struggle from the 19th century." He argues, too, that the whole hunting debate in Britain is linked to the "increasing polarization between an intolerant, even aggressive urban society and a traditional rural society", a split that countries like Spain, Ireland, France and the Nordic nations have escaped because of much closer links between countryside and town.

If foxhunting is to go, shooting could follow, and on cruelty grounds, fishing should go too – though the government has been at pains to say these two sports are safe. There are lots of votes in-fishermen and, besides, fishermen don't look down their noses from high horses.

From: *TIME,* 1st April 2002

1 toff: a disapproving way of referring to somebody from a high social class

2 Yves Lecoq: secretary-general of the Brussels-based E.U. Federation of Associations for Hunting and Conservation

## Lösungsvorschlag

### I. Questions on the text

1. First of all, the decision was democratic because the Labour Party clearly kept its promise to let the MPs vote on a ban, which it had made in its 1997 election manifesto. Secondly, before they voted the issue was thoroughly discussed in newspapers and displayed on billboards. Also the Home Secretary had called for an impartial investigation. Thirdly, the vote was free in the sense that the MPs were not forced to vote according to the party line but they could follow their consciences. And finally, it was not a simple "yes or no" vote but they could vote on four different proposals.

2. The author states that the trouble with all democratic decisions is that they may restrict the liberty of minorities. And in this case it is a fairly large minority that cares very much about its sport. Moreover, he refers to the Burns report, which stated that hunting was still the best method for controlling the fox population, that a lot of people would become unemployed if foxhunting were banned, and finally that a ban would thoroughly change the rural way of life, as foxhunting is one of the activities that unites the people.

3. *In line 44 the writer quotes the MPs' argument that foxhunting is cruel and must therefore be legislated. Proceeding from that statement he develops his argumentation in lines 47 to 53.*

   The author admits that foxhunting is cruel but does not believe this is a convincing argument to justify the ban. If you do not draw a line somewhere you can also ban shooting, fishing, animal experiments and the slaughtering of other animals on the same grounds. But the line you draw must not infringe upon human liberty, which it does in this case.
   Moreover, as foxhunting only accounts for a small number of foxes that are killed every year, a ban would even inflict more cruelty on the animals: to limit their number, people would resort to other methods, such as shooting or snaring.

4. The third paragraph reverses the author's argumentation: so far he seems to have made the case for a ban on foxhunting, pointing out how democratic the whole process has been. Explicitly repeating that the whole process was "a perfect demonstration of democracy", he then surprises the reader by stating: "That is the whole trouble." (l. 28). The next sentence introduces his main concern, i. e. that democracy may endanger the liberty of minorities, which it does in this case. This statement is the more effective as the writer uses the very words of the first part – it was a *"perfect demonstration"* of democracy (ll. 27/28) but it also *"demonstrated perfectly"* (l. 28) that it *"seriously compromises* the liberty of minorities" (l. 29), which echoes his earlier statement that foxhunting *"seriously compromises* the welfare of the fox." (l. 18).

5. *The present text contains numerous sideswipes at both sides to make it clear that the debate has been rather "malicious" (l. 4). The writer states for example that both sides plastered "lurid photographs convenient to their respective arguments ... over newspapers and billboards." (l. 15) In line 6 he calls the statements of some of the supporters of foxhunting "yelps". If you read carefully you will find more passages that confirm this view.*

   The writer insinuates that a lot of MPs voted with regard to their personal profit rather than their consciences when he states that they followed "at least their individual calculations." (ll. 20/21) Moreover, he accuses some opponents of foxhunting of not wanting to see the other side when he says that they "simply refuse to acknowledge" (ll. 30/31) that a ban would mean a restriction of liberty or when he quotes the Labour

Party as dismissing foxhunting as a "so-called sport" (l. 35) or city dwellers seeing it as "sadistic pastime of the rich" (l. 42)
But it is not only the opponents who are criticized. The "shriller advocates [utter] yelps" (l. 6), i. e. are hysterical about the debate. Like their opponents, they take a rather sensational approach to the matter, plastering "lurid photographs convenient to their respective arguments […] over newspapers and billboards." (ll. 14/15). Moreover, they exaggerate the consequences of a ban for "rural jobs and the rural way of life" (ll. 36/37).

6. *Note that the writer takes the threat to the liberty of minorities very seriously ("democracy seriously compromises the liberty of minorities", l. 29) whereas he is rather ironic or even sarcastic when it comes to the fate of the foxes ("Of the 400,000 or so foxes […] few expire peacefully in bed", ll. 54/55) Don't forget that you have to analyze tone* ***and*** *language.*

   When the writer deals with the behaviour of the people involved in the debate or with the fate of the foxes, he employs a rather **humorous** and **ironic tone**, which sometimes becomes rather **sarcastic**, especially when he tries to expose the MPs' motivation for their decision: "MPs were allowed to vote in accordance with their individual consciences (or at least their individual calculations)" (ll. 20/21). The effect is heightened by the alliteration of the noble idea of "conscience" and the rather low-minded "calculations". His choice of words further exposes the behaviour of the opponents when he says that they "*marshalled*" (instead of organized) their arguments and *"plastered"* lurid photographs over newspapers and billboards. He also uses extended metaphors, for example when he speaks about Shadow Home Secretary Ann Widdecombe, who "consulted a *furry corner* of her *steely heart"* (l. 25).
   When the writer deals with his main issue, namely the liberty of minorities, his tone becomes rather serious. He often uses short, laconic and apodictic sentences to make his point: "… liberty is the pre-eminent issue." (ll. 31/32); "That is the whole trouble." (l. 28); "It just happens to be wrong." (ll. 63/64)

## II. Composition

1. **"Democracy is the worst form of government except all those other forms that have been tried from time to time." (Winston Churchill). Do you agree with this statement?**

   *Please note what Churchill wants to say with his paradoxical remark: if it is the worst form of government except all others, it is in fact the best but by no means perfect. What you can do here is first mention all the drawbacks of democracy you can think of (long process to make decisions, sluggishness in carrying out reforms, etc.) before you point out its undeniable advantages.*

   Ever since the fall of the Communist regimes in Eastern Europe in the early 1990s democracy has been on the uprise in the world. Judging by the development of the West European countries after the Second World War, democracy seems indeed to be an ideal form of government that guarantees economic success. It has indeed been much better than any other form of government, be it authoritarian, totalitarian or even theocratic.
   So what did Churchill have in mind when he said it was by no means perfect? Perhaps he had in mind that the German democracy of the Weimar Republic had enabled Hitler's rise to dictatorship. Or he simply thought of the obvious disadvantages of the political process in democracies: decision-making takes too long, people are only superficially informed about the issues they have to vote on. Moreover, it seems to be very difficult in democracies to carry out reforms because political pressure groups try

to preserve their privileges. Finally, politicians try to provide their voters with short-term advantages rather than long-term solutions because the latter can't be turned into votes.

In spite of all these weaknesses, however, no other system can claim to be better. No other form of government gives people as much say in public affairs as democracy. Moreover, we must not forget that true participation in decisions requires freedom for the individual. And as real freedom is indivisible every democratic state must protect its minorities and guarantee their well-being.

As all this is an integral part of the system and not just granted by a condescending king or a benevolent dictator it is true that democracy is the best form of government that has ever been tested.

2. **"The credibility of any political system depends on how it deals with minorities." Discuss.**

   "Freedom is indivisible, and when one man is enslaved, all are not free." Those were John F. Kennedy's words in his famous Berlin speech on June 26, 1963. This sentence really describes democracy in a nutshell: a society that provides freedom only for a – however sizeable – majority, cannot really be called a free society.

   Quite a few people see democracy simply as majority rule. The majority decides and the minority has to comply, they think. If fifty-one percent decide on a matter, the rest of the nation has to follow suit. However, this can easily develop into a dictatorship, a tyranny of the majority. Before Rosa Parks refused to give up her seat to a white man in a municipal bus in Montgomery, Al., the majority in the south had decided that segregation and with it discrimination of blacks was right. It is also very likely that a majority of Germans agreed when Hitler began to deprive the Jews of their rights as citizens, even though they may have been against their extermination. But that is just the point: if you accept everything the majority decides, you may easily end up persecuting the minorities, be they sexual, religious, or racial. That is why freedom should always be "the freedom of those who think differently", as Rosa Luxemburg put it.

   The rule of the majority may be a political device to obtain a political decision without the use of force, but to be credible a democracy as well as any political system must also have constitutional limits on governments, equality of all citizens, and above all it must guarantee the rights of minorities. If those rights are not observed, then – as Kennedy put it – "all are not free".

3. **Is the liberty of the hunter a higher value than the right to life of the hunted?**

   *Note that the subject is a really "hot potato" between animal-rights activits and hunters. Activists have recently gone so far as to compare hunting to the Nazi Holocaust, whereas hunters tend to point out that they do not kill for fun but claim liberty for what they call "a useful service to society". It depends on your personal view how you decide on that matter.*

   Hunting has recently come under heavy attack. Members of radical animal-rights groups, who want to ban hunting altogether, say that animals should enjoy the right to "life, liberty, and the pursuit of happiness" just like human beings. Total animal liberation means to them that animals are to be treated exactly like human beings. That means of course that all farming, fishing and, above all, hunting animals must be banned, because they "cause pain, trauma, and grief to both the victims and the survivors", as PETA[1] puts it. Hunting, they say, is simply a form of recreation for an influential minority that should not have priority over the rights of those creatures that are incapable of asserting their rights. I think not only hunters would disagree with these views. Most people would point out that men have hunted since prehistoric times and that the "sport" of hunting has not only a grand tradition but also does a useful

service to society by keeping the animal population under control. You cannot expect nature to limit the number of deer in our populated areas; if left alone, the animals would probably eat crops in the fields or invade people's lawns. You can easily imagine the fate of the animals considering the farmers' and house owners' anger.
There may be hunters who hunt for fun, or because hunting adds to their social prestige, or even because they want to put antlers[2] as trophies on their walls, but like in all other fields of life a few black sheep do not discredit the majority of responsible hunters.
Society must protect their liberty. But at the same time it must also find safeguards against excessive hunting as well as against cruelty to animals. With such a complicated question the answer cannot be that one side is of more value than the other but it must be more balanced.

Anmerkungen
1 PETA – People for the Ethical Treatment of Animals, a worldwide operating animal-rights group
2 antlers – dt. „Geweih"

4. **At a fashion show an animal-rights activist has thrown bags of paint at a model presenting a fur coat.**
**You have interviewed this activist. Write up the interview for publication in your magazine.**

*This task marks the beginning of a new form of composition in the Bavarian Abitur, which wants to offer a greater variety of assignments. Remember that you should conduct the interview by first asking the activist questions about his views and background before you go into detail and ask him why he resorted to violence, e. g. attacking a model with bags of paint.*

QUESTION: Michael, you threw those bags of paint against a model at the fashion show last Saturday to protest against the violation of animal rights. Why did you become an animal-rights activist in the first place?

ANSWER: Well, you know, I have been a vegetarian for a long time. At first I thought that was the best way of protesting against our way of keeping animals. But then it dawned on me that animals have the same rights as human beings and all exploiting of other species is unethical.

QUESTION*:* Are you a member of any organization supporting animal rights?

ANSWER: Well, yes, at first I joined the Royal Society for the Prevention of Cruelty to Animals. We did really a lot of activities, published articles about animal rights, protested in the streets, but soon I noticed that we did not achieve much. That was when I first heard of PETA, which stands for People for the Ethical Treatment of Animals and fights for nothing less than "total animal liberation".

QUESTION: I see, but why did you throw those bags of paint at the model in the fur coat? Couldn't you have protested more peacefully?

ANSWER: As I just said, I was disappointed with those well-behaved groups which never achieved anything. What could I have done? Holding up a banner? Nobody – let me tell you, not a single person would have noticed that and so we wouldn't have achieved anything. But as soon as you break the rules the papers are full of it and people will begin taking an interest in our group and its aims. So, I hope you see I had to throw these bags because it's the only way to change the world.

QUESTION: Michael, thank you very much for this interview.

## III. Translation

Viele Briten fragen sich, worum es bei der ganzen Aufregung geht. Warum ist gerade die Fuchsjagd die Streitfrage, die – angesichts der Tatsache, dass das öffentliche Verkehrssystem zerfällt, dass die Krankenhäuser überlastet sind, dass die Schulen versagen und die ländlichen Gegenden von den Verwüstungen der Maul- und Klauenseuche heimgesucht werden[1] – die parlamentarischen Leidenschaften wirklich erregt.

Könnte das wahre Motiv hinter dem Verbot des Sports Gehässigkeit sein, eine Möglichkeit, es diesen Schnöseln auf dem Rücken ihrer Pferde zu zeigen[2], ein letztes Aufbäumen des Klassenkampfes? (Und sogar diese Meinung ist unangebracht, da die Hälfte der Jäger wohl Ladenbesitzer und Kleinbauern sind.) Das ist die Ansicht von Yves Lecocq, und er sagt, dass ein Verbot viele Europäer davon überzeugen wird, dass „die britische Gesellschaft den Klassenkampf des 19. Jahrhunderts noch nicht überwunden hat." Er behauptet[3] auch, dass die ganze Debatte über die Jagd, die in Großbritannien geführt wird, mit der „zunehmenden Aufspaltung des Landes[4] in eine intolerante, sogar aggressive städtische Gesellschaft und eine traditionsgebundene ländliche Gesellschaft" zusammenhängt, eine Trennung, die Ländern wie Spanien, Irland, Frankreich und den nordischen Nationen wegen viel engerer Bindungen zwischen Stadt und Land erspart geblieben ist.

Wenn die Fuchsjagd abgeschafft werden sollte, könnte es der Jagd überhaupt[5] ebenso ergehen, und wegen seiner Grausamkeit sollte auch das Fischen abgeschafft werden – obwohl die Regierung sich große Mühe gegeben hat, zu versichern, dass diese beiden Sportarten nicht zur Debatte stehen[6]. Bei den Fischern gibt es viele Stimmen zu holen[7], und außerdem sitzen sie nicht auf dem hohen Ross[8] und blicken hochnäsig auf einen herab[9].

Anmerkungen

1 Da „to devastate" (= verwüsten) und „ravage" (= Verwüstung) dasselbe ausdrücken, braucht man im Deutschen ein anderes Verb.

2 to get at s.o. – wörtl.: auf jdn. losgehen

3 „argumentiert" ist natürlich auch richtig

4 Zusatz zur Verdeutlichung. „Polarisierung" ist ebenfalls möglich

5 „shooting" bezieht sich hier auf die Jagd mit dem Gewehr, d. h. ohne die für die Fuchsjagd typischen Hunde

6 wörtl.: „sicher sind"

7 Zusatz zur Verdeutlichung

8 „to be on one's high horse" ist ein bildhafter Ausdruck und bedeutet wie im Deutschen „auf dem hohen Ross sitzen"

9 „to look down one's nose at ..." – = dt. „die Nase rümpfen über"; „hochnäsig herabblicken auf"

## Leistungskurs Englisch 2003
## Textaufgabe II

**T. C. Boyle, *The Tortilla Curtain,* 1995**

América found him at the bottom of the path, bundled in the twilight like a heap of rags. She'd walked nearly eight miles already, down out of the canyon to the highway along the ocean where she could catch the bus to Venice[1] for a sewing job that never materialized, and then back again, and she was like death on two feet. Two dollars and twenty cents down the drain and nothing to show for it. In the morning, at first light, she'd walked along the Coast Highway, and that made her feel good, made her feel like a girl again – the salt smell, people jogging on the beach, the amazing narrow-shouldered houses of the millionaires growing up like mushrooms out of the sand – but the address the Guatemalan woman had given her was worth nothing. All the way there, all the way out in the alien world, a neighbourhood, drunks in the street, and the building was boarded up, deserted, no back entrance, no sewing machines, no hard-faced boss to stand over her and watch her sweat at three dollars and thirty-five cents an hour, no nothing. She checked the address twice, three times, and then she turned round to retrace her steps and found that the streets had shuffled themselves in the interim, and she knew she was lost.

By lunchtime, she could taste the panic in the back of her throat. For the first time in four months, for the first time since they'd left the South and her village and everything she knew in the world, she was separated from Cándido. She walked in circles and everything looked strange, even when she'd seen it twice, three times over. She didn't speak the language. Black people sauntered up the street with plastic grocery bags dangling from their wrists. She stepped in dog excrement. A *gabacho*[2] sat on the sidewalk with his long hair and begged for change and the sight of him struck her with unholy terror: If he had to beg in his own country, what chance was there for her? But she held on to her six little silvery coins and finally a woman with the *chilango* accent of Mexico City helped her find the bus.

She had to walk back up the canyon in the bleak light of the declining day while the cars swished by her in a lethal hissing chain, and in every one a pair of eyes that screamed, *Get out, get out of here and go back where you belong!* – and how long before one of them tore up the dirt in front of her and the police were standing there demanding her papers? She hurried along, head down, shoulders thrust forward, and when the strip of pavement at the side of the road narrowed to six inches she had to climb over the guardrail and plow[3] through the brush.

Sweat stung her eyes. Burrs and thorns and the smooth hard daggers of the foxtails[4] bit into every step. She couldn't see where she was going. She worried about snakes, spiders, turning her ankle in a ditch. And then the cars began to switch on their lights and she was alone on a terrible howling stage, caught there for everyone to see. Her clothes were soaked through by the time the entrance to the path came into sight, and she ran the last hundred yards, ran for the cover of the brush while the cold beams of light hunted her down, and she had to crouch there in the bushes till her breath came back to her.

The shadows deepened. Birds called to one another. *Swish, swish, swish,* the cars shot by, no more than ten feet away. Any one of them could stop, any one. She listened to the cars and to the air rasping through her lips, to the hiss of the tires and the metallic whine of the engines straining against the grade. It went on for a long time, forever, and the sky grew darker. Finally, when she was sure no one was following her, she started down the path, letting the trees and the shrubs and the warm breath of the night calm her, hungry now – ravenous – and so thirsty she could drink up the whole streambed, whether Cándido thought the water was safe or not.

At first, the thing in the path wasn't anything to concern her – a shape, a concert of shades, light and dark – and then it was a rock, a pile of laundry, and finally, a man, her man, sleeping there in the dirt. Her first thought was that he was drunk – he'd got work and he'd been drinking, drinking cold beer and wine while she struggled through the nine circles of Hell – and she felt the rage come up in her. No lunch – she hadn't had a bite since dawn, and then it was only a burned tortilla and an egg – and nothing to drink even, not so much as a sip of water. What did he think she was? But then she bent and touched him and she knew that she was in the worst trouble of her life.



1 Venice: town near Los Angeles
2 *gabacho: Spanish:* derogatory term for a white American of European descent
3 to plow: US spelling of "to plough"
4 foxtail: name of a plant; long, dry kind of grass

**Worksheet:**

maximum number of points attainable

## I. Questions on the text

Read all the questions first, then answer them in the given order. Use your own words as far as is appropriate.

1. Who is América? Sum up what the reader learns about her origins, her social background and her situation in the US. — 20
2. Why does América go to Venice and what does she experience there? — 20
3. Examine América's behaviour and feelings on her way "back up the canyon" (l. 26) before she finds her husband. — 20
4. Analyse four examples of different ways in which the author uses language to convey América's state of mind in lines 33 to 47. — 20
5. Give a detailed description of América's reactions and thoughts in the final paragraph. How does this paragraph relate to the very beginning of the excerpt? — 20

## II. Composition

Choose *one* of the following topics. Write about 250 to 300 words. — 50

1. Earlier Immigrants to the US usually tried to learn English as quickly as possible; today many Hispanics insist on using their mother tongue. Discuss the consequences this new phenomenon might have.
2. Tourists and immigrants – can their experiences in a foreign country be compared?
3. Does literature have the power to change society?

4. More and more exclusive residential areas in the US are becoming gated communities, walled and guarded to keep out "undesirable elements of society".
Exville, California, is considering such a change and has invited all the property owners to an important meeting. You are one of these property owners and feel you have to convince a majority of your position. Write down your speech.

## III. Translation

Translate the following text into German: 50/200

The rise in immigration and its changing composition after 1970 renewed the ambivalence and even hostility that Americans felt towards immigrants. Given the rate of immigration, averaging about one million annually in the 1990s, and high birth rates among Latinos[1], projections suggested that by 2050 Hispanics[1] would rise to 25 percent of the United States population, while whites would shrink to a bare majority. Sounding much like Theodore Roosevelt during World War I, Patrick J. Buchanan, the politician most concerned publicly about immigration, warned in 1994 that the United States was heading for social fragmentation: "If America is to survive as 'one nation, one people', we need to call a timeout on immigration to assimilate the tens of millions who have lately arrived."

The sluggish economy of the late 1980s and early 1990s, especially in California, helped fuel Americans' fears about the economic effects of immigration. Yet the initial impetus for a new immigration debate and movement to restrict the number of newcomers came from environmentalists, who were dissatisfied that groups like the Sierra Club[1] did not take positions favoring cuts in the migrant flow. They believed that too many people were coming to America and that the country's natural resources could not sustain a population growing at such a rate.

From: Leonard Dinnerstein, *Ethnic Americans: a History of Immigration.* New York: New York University Press 1999

1 nicht übersetzen

## Lösungsvorschlag

### I. Questions on the text (American spelling)

*The clues for your answer are to be found throughout the text. We recommend that you mark them and then assemble them under three headings before you put them together in your own words.*

| origins | social background | situation |
| --- | --- | --- |
| • the Sout<br>• chilango accent | • village<br>• didn't speak the language<br>• Cándido | • death on two feet<br>• 2 dollars and 20 cents down<br>• the chain<br>• her coins<br>• demanding her papers<br>• canyon<br>• hadn't had a bite |

1. América is from "the South", probably from Mexico City, as she is familiar with the *chilango* accent. Four months ago she left her native village, which is all she has known of the world. She speaks no English. With her companion or husband Cándido she seems to be camping in a canyon in extreme poverty – she only had a frugal breakfast, eats and drinks nothing during the day and is unhappy to have to spend the little money she has on the bus fare. Her fear of the police indicates that she is an illegal immigrant.

2. A Guatemalan woman has given her an address where she can find a job as a seamstress. She goes there full of hope even though the wages will be poor and enjoys the journey and the views. But when she discovers that the shop has been closed down she begins to despair and notices the shabbiness of this "alien world" (l. 10) and the bad neighborhood. She loses her orientation and starts walking in circles. The sight of a white American begging in his own country depresses her because it makes her realize how scant her own chances are of making a living as an illegal immigrant.

3. *Don't forget to examine her behavior and her feelings. Both points are connected in the text. You will find the answers in ll. 29 to 53.*

   On her way back to the canyon América feels persecuted by the rapidly passing cars on the highway. She imagines that the eyes of the drivers "scream" at her to "get back where you belong" (l. 27) and dreads the prospect of being stopped by a state trooper and being arrested as an undocumented immigrant. So she walks faster, "head down" (l. 30) like a hunted animal sweating and worrying about snakes and spiders and the danger of injuring her ankle. It gets darker and she feels exposed by the sweeping headlights of the cars. She begins to run for the shelter of the bushes to rest there and hide until she feels safer. When her fear that a car might stop abates, she continues her walk, much more at ease now and comforted by the trees and bushes and the warmth of the night. Now she realizes how extremely hungry and thirsty she is.

4. *The passage in question is rich in poetic uses of language. Be aware that the task calls for four different stylistic devices. Here are some examples in the order in which they appear:*

| | |
|---|---|
| "smooth hard daggers … bit" (l. 33) | metaphor, personification |
| "terrible howling stage" (l. 36) | choice of adjective, metaphor, personification |
| "ran … ran" (l. 37 f.) | repetition |
| "cold beams of light hunted her" (l. 38) | choice of adjective, personification |
| "Swish, swish, swish" (l. 40) | repetition, onomatopoeia |
| "Any one … any one" (l. 41) | repetition |
| "hiss … whine" (l. 42) | suggestive verbs, (snakes, wolves) |
| "a long time, forever" (l. 43) | climax, exaggeration |
| "warm breath of the night" (l. 45) | positive adjective, personification |
| "hungry now – ravenous" (l. 45 f.) | climax |
| "the whole streambed" (l. 46) | exaggeration |

The text abounds in figures of speech and poetic language, which illustrate and intensify América's feelings. I have chosen the following four examples:

1) She was "alone on a terrible howling stage" (l. 33): this expression combines a metaphor (she feels as if she was on a stage) with a personification (the stage howls). These images together with the negative adjective "terrible" depict América's sense of utter loneliness and exposure to the hostile drivers passing by. The cars' headlights are like searchlights that leave her no chance to hide.
2) "ran … ran" (l. 37 f.): This repetition underlines her panic and her frantic attempt to escape from what she imagines to be her pursuers.
3) "a long time, forever" (l. 43): The climax of "forever" and the exaggeration of this expression emphasize that she feels her ordeal to be everlasting and she is almost beyond hope that it might come to an end.
4) "warm breath of the night" (l. 45): The positive adjective and the personification of the night as a being that can give the "breath of life" calming and healing her after her dreadful experiences mark a short period of rest and hope before América faces a new terror.

5. *Mind that this is a triple question: reactions, thoughts, relation between beginning and ending.*

At first América approaches the "shape" without misgivings, until she discovers the truth: her husband lies on the ground, lifeless. Her initial assumption is that he is drunk, which evokes her hot anger – how can he allow himself to get drunk while she has had this horrible day, with nothing to eat or drink since her meager breakfast! How can he be so inconsiderate and selfish! But when she touches him it dawns on her that Cándido is far from being drunk, and her fury turns into despair and fear and she is convinced that "the worst trouble of her life" (l. 55) has begun.
The final paragraph continues from the first sentence of the text, which at first stands isolated from the following narration but is explained in the final paragraph. Thus the beginning and the ending serve as a frame.

## II. Composition

### 1. Discuss the consequences of many Hispanics insisting on using their mother tongue.

Canada seems to be thriving with the existence of two language groups, without visible ill effects. Could this not also happen in the US?

If bilingualism should be accepted by US society it could open the doors for greater cultural variety in literature, film and customs. Many people would become interested in learning Spanish and travel to Latin America. The position of the hitherto discriminated against Hispanic minority would be strengthened and increase their identification with their new home country. In addition, closer economic and political relations with the South would be reinforced.

On the other hand the problems cannot be ignored. There is still a considerable hostility by the Anglo majority to the establishment of a second, Spanish-speaking culture and a deep resentment by the Hispanics to the intolerance of public and official America. Some US citizens fear that already existing language ghettoes could be blown up out of proportion and further deepen the rift between Anglos and Latinos. The current economic sectors are overwhelmingly English speaking and would be practically closed to Latinos, thereby increasing their levels of unemployment. If bilingualism would become the rule separate facilities for Latinos would become necessary: schools, universities, hospitals – and it is difficult to imagine how the US armed forces could function with mixed personnel. The acceptance of a second official language would also mean that laws, road signs, or product labels would have to be translated.

All in all, it looks as if the problems would be much more serious than in Canada, where the Franco-Canadian minority is limited to one province. The necessary tolerance of the Anglos is not yet in sight. The only solution is the acceptance of two (and more) cultures within the framework of the English language.

### 2. Tourists and immigrants – can their experiences be compared?

*As this topic calls for a comparison it is a good idea to first look up the definitions for tourist and immigrant in your dictionary.*

*tourist: someone who is traveling or visiting a place for pleasure (DCE); immigrant: someone who comes from abroad to live permanently in another country (DCE)*

International tourists and immigrants both come to a country from abroad, the first in search of pleasure, the latter to live there permanently. It is an interesting question whether their experiences are comparable at all.

The tourist selects his country of destination considering its recreation value, cultural interest, climate and affordability. He may want to laze on sunny Spanish beaches, stay in reasonably priced hotels, and dine in restaurants with delicious menus. Others may prefer to hike along the Inca Trail in Peru or marvel at the Chinese Wall. The tourists can normally count on the natives being welcoming and hospitable and treating them as guests. To some extent they contribute to the country's economic welfare by spending their money on accommodation, food and souvenirs.

Immigrants, more often than not, are rarely in a position to be choosy with respect to their new place of residence. Frequently their prospects in their home countries are hopeless; they expect finally to make a decent living in the new one. Often the natives are hostile, especially if the immigrants belong to the unskilled, impoverished classes, because they compete for jobs with the local people. This is the case of Latinos in the US, who arrive in great numbers and hardly speak a word of English. What kind of treatment can you expect as an unwelcome and unwanted intruder? They are discriminated against in their search for homes, work, and social acceptance; they will be harassed by the authorities as potential illegal aliens.

It is plain to see that the experiences of tourists and immigrants cannot really be compared. It makes a big difference whether you pay a friendly visit to a country for a limited time, or whether you have come to stay fighting your way against great odds in a mostly hostile environment. Tourists are encouraged to return, immigrants are resented – until they become natives as well.

3. **Does literature have the power to change society?**

Good literature in the form of novels, plays, or poetry is not only somebody's way of making a living by selling his products, it is also an artistic expression of the author's view of the world, which sometimes makes a strong case for his readers to re-examine existing conditions. But can such an appeal also have the power to change society?
Cultural pessimists would hold that most literature is trash and only contributes to cementing people's blissful ignorance by confirming their trivial beliefs – boy meets girl, love triumphs, all goes well, honesty will be rewarded, heroes are invulnerable, criminals will be brought to justice. Books by popular writers like Rosamunde Pilcher or Tom Clancy only try to entertain their readers and never call for changes.
And yet some authors come to mind whose novels have deeply moved their readers. Charles Dickens, with his portrayals of the miserable living-conditions of the poor, as in Oliver Twist, was a social critic who helped to strengthen the feeling of human solidarity in Victorian England. His American contemporary, Harriet Beecher Stowe, made a much greater and more immediate impact with her "Uncle Tom's Cabin". This tremendously successful book raised a public outcry for the abolition of slavery in the US, which partly caused the Civil War. To Abraham Lincoln she was the little woman who made this great war.
It looks as if literature normally has little effect, but may influence individual readers' opinions and, in rare cases, does have the power to change society.

4. **Write a speech to convince a majority of your position regarding the establishment of a gated community.**

*This topic is the beginning of a new composition format in the Bavarian Abitur where more creative assignments are offered. In this particular topic you can follow the pattern of the argumentative essay. See also Textaufgabe I, question 4.*

Ladies and gentlemen, friends and neighbors,

We have come together to make an important decision for our community – whether to protect our neighborhood with fences and gates against undesirable elements, or to remain as we are, with free access for everybody to our streets and residences.
We wouldn't have gathered here if we didn't have good reason to be concerned about the safety of our families and homes. Breakins have occurred here and there, strangers have used our parks as barbecue grounds, and job seekers and salespersons ring our doorbells. This could indeed be reduced by walling ourselves in, with checkpoints at our gates and security patrols within the area.
I am sure we could bear the costs which security constructions and maintenance would entail – but what about the non-material consequences? Do we really want to live in a gilded cage and close ourselves off from the humbler members of society? Has it come to this that our cherished American way of life can only survive if we protect it with armed guards and battlements? America has always been the land of the free and has always succeeded in defending its values and its security without resorting to restrictions and distrust. It is a fact that not even the mighty Chinese Wall prevented intruders when the civil spirit of those protected slackened.
Let us therefore not overreact and remain open to the world outside and protect our safety, as we have always done, by sensible, traditional and democratic means. This is not to say that one day we should not reconsider such a decision. But for the time be-

ing I strongly feel that our liberty is at stake, and that we still can handle the occasional 'undesirable element'. I move that we rest the case today and meet again if we think we can't give normality another chance.

## III. Translation

Der Anstieg der Einwanderung und ihre sich verändernde Zusammensetzung nach 1970 erneuerten die gemischten und sogar feindseligen Gefühle[1] der Amerikaner gegenüber Einwanderern. Auf der Basis der Immigrationsrate[2] der neunziger Jahre, die im Schnitt etwa eine Million jährlich betrug, und den hohen Geburtenziffern bei den Latinos, ergaben Hochrechnungen, dass bis 2050 die Hispanics auf einen Anteil von 25 % der Bevölkerung der Vereinigten Staaten anwachsen würden, während gleichzeitig[3] die Weißen bis auf eine hauchdünne Mehrheit schrumpfen würden. Patrick J. Buchanan, der Politiker, der sich öffentlich höchst besorgt über die Einwanderung auslässt, warnte 1994 davor – und hörte sich ganz wie Theodore Roosevelt während des 1. Weltkriegs an – dass die Vereinigten Staaten auf eine gesellschaftliche Zersplitterung zusteuerten: „Wenn Amerika als ‚eine Nation, ein Volk' überleben soll, müssen wir eine Auszeit für die Einwanderung ausrufen, um die mehreren zehn Millionen einzugliedern, die in letzter Zeit angekommen sind."

Die vor allem in Kalifornien schwächelnde Wirtschaft der späten achtziger und frühen neunziger Jahre trug dazu bei, die Ängste der Amerikaner vor den wirtschaftlichen Auswirkungen der Zuwanderung zu schüren. Der eigentliche Anstoß für eine neue Einwanderungsdebatte und eine politische[4] Bewegung mit dem Ziel, die Zahl der Neuzugänge zu begrenzen, kam jedoch von Umweltschützern, die unzufrieden damit waren, dass Gruppen wie der Sierra Club sich nicht stark machten[5] für Einschnitte beim Einwanderungsstrom. Sie glaubten, dass zu viele Leute nach Amerika kämen und dass die Schätze der Natur[6] ein Bevölkerungswachstum dieses Ausmaßes nicht verkraften könnten.

Anmerkungen

1 wörtlich: zwiespältige Haltung und Feindseligkeit

2 *immigration* kommt häufig vor, daher kann man zur Abwechslung auch einmal Immigration oder Zuwanderung schreiben

3 stilistisch bedingte Einfügung, welche die Gegensätzlichkeit von *while* verstärkt

4 Einfügung zur Verdeutlichung

5 Die wörtliche Übersetzung (die keine Positionen bezogen, die Einschnitte befürworteten) klingt umständlich

6 *natural resources:* Naturschätze. Bodenschätze ist hier nicht logisch, da für deren Ausbeutung sehr wohl neue Arbeitskräfte gebraucht würden, wird aber wahrscheinlich auch akzeptiert.

**Leistungskurs Englisch 2004**
**Textaufgabe I**

## The right to be beautiful

Of course, it is ridiculous. What sane person would put metal rings round her neck to stretch it like a giraffe's, or lace her corset so tight that she fainted, or allow her feet to be bound to make them tiny? How backward, how primitive. Completely different, obviously, from the woman who pays huge sums to have her breasts surgically enlarged; or the man who takes drugs to give him an athlete's torso; or the rich, modern men and women who spend $160 billion a year on beauty products whose impact on the appearance is sometimes, um, unproven. From stilettos to diets to cosmetic surgery, women (and, increasingly, men) go to great lengths and huge cost to make themselves better looking. And now, advances in technology allow people to change their appearance not just for an evening out but for ever.

Does it matter if human beings change their bodies in more fundamental ways than our grandparents ever dreamt of? The reasons for change go well beyond the pursuit of beauty, of course. Athletes reshape themselves to do better at sport, but it is beauty that dominates the remodelling business and that raises the toughest questions.

The search for beauty has always seemed frivolous to some. Puritans, who once squawked about the evils of lipstick and facepaint, now have fresh moral dilemmas to wrestle with. If the beauty business deceives people into spending money uselessly or harmfully, should it be stopped from doing so? Some fret that the preoccupation with appearance is leading to a shallower society, and to a host of social horrors from family breakdown to eating disorders. Others fear that beauty firms are trying to blur the line between drugs and cosmetics, or complain that tampering with the incline of one's nose is the first step on a slippery slope to tampering with one's genes.

Only in the case of the young are there grounds for special intervention – although parental responsibility ought really to do the job. Until their bodies stop growing, teenagers should not be allowed to change them in permanent ways that may turn out to be harmful. By all means straighten their teeth and even their noses, but leave puppy fat alone. Let them pierce their ears or indeed their tongues, if they must, but ban the tattoos and hold that graduation present of breast enlargement.

But what of adults, who behave little more rationally than teenagers in this regard? Perhaps governments should get the makers of those creams made of dolphin serum and goose fat to list the ingredients on the pot, as if they were breakfast cereals. Big beauty companies, experts at deception, have the money and power to play on people's hopes and fears. As for the poor, sales of beauty products tend to take off when incomes rise. Lipstick may be an indicator of economic progress. And the freedom to believe nonsense about getting rid of wrinkles is one of the most basic human liberties.

The more difficult question will arise when it becomes clear that some of the promises actually come true. Good-looking people have great advantages over the ugly. For example, they earn more: when Barry Harper of London Guildhall University looked at 11,000 British 33-year-olds, he found that the pay penalty for unattractiveness was around 15 % for men and 11 % for women. Overweight women earned 5 % less than average, especially in clerical and secretarial jobs. Good looks in both sexes mattered especially in sales jobs, where the seller meets the buyer.

Not only do looks help in the job market. In both sexes, they help in the marriage market. Studies show that handsome folk are more confident. It is a cruel fact that good looks can make you a better parent: babies are attracted to prettier people. Good looks remove some of life's irritations: people rated as more attractive feel more entitled to better treatment and are less willing to be kept waiting; good-looking women with a flat tyre get rescued first. And a nice face helps to get people out of trouble: a recent study found that university student awarded criminals sentences which were 20 % lighter if they were told that the villains were "handsome" or "pretty".

If a bit of lipstick can keep you out of jail, or waxing your moustache can land an extra 15 % in earnings, then who would not pay for successful beauty treatments? If genetic engineering ever catches on, it will be hard to draw a firm line between correcting defects and enhancing characteristics. It would be irrational for parents who love their children not to want them to be more beautiful as well as healthier and more intelligent.

But if society believes that government should aim to give citizens equal opportunities, might beauty be a right that society can be legitimately asked to pay for? The poor once looked very different from the rich: they were worse fed, worse clothed, worse washed and had less access to medical and dental care. Those days are gone, at least in the developed world. But bat ears or a cleft lip can still make a teenager's life a misery. The World Health Organisation has broadened its definition of health to include psychological well-being. Stand by for the moment when public policy has cut out the most striking sources of inequality, and conventions of cosmetic surgeons announce that their craft can excise the remainder.

From: *The Economist*, 24 May 2002

**Worksheet:**

maximum number of points attainable

## I. Questions on the text

Read all the questions first, then answer them in the given order. Use your own words as far as is appropriate.

1. People have always taken measures to change their outward appearance. Outline the development of these changes. — 10
2. Summarize the arguments against cosmetic changes and the search for beauty. — 20
3. What reasons make the pursuit of physical enhancement comprehensible or justifiable? Give evidence from the text. — 20
4. In the whole spectrum of attempts to change one's appearance, with whom should the responsibility lie? — 10
5. Compare the ideas of the final paragraph with what is implied in the title. — 20
6. How does the writer use tone and language to convey his attitude? Analyse four examples. — 20

## II. Composition

Choose *one* of the following topics. Write about 250 to 300 words. — 50

1. "Every generation laughs at the old fashions, but follows religiously the new" (Henry David Thoreau, 1817–1862). Comment on this statement.

2. "The surest way to corrupt a youth is to instruct him to hold in higher esteem those who think alike than those who think differently" (Friedrich Nietzsche, 1844–1900). Comment on this statement.
3. Your school magazine is doing an English-language dossier on tattoos. You contribute by writing an article.
4. A reporter talks to an athlete who has tested positive for illegal substances. Write up the interview published in a sports magazine.

## III. Translation

Translate the following text into German: 50
200

The brain is just as much a muscle as any other part of the body; and the more you exercise it, the more vigorous and robust it gets. But the corollary of this is that people who don't keep on challenging themselves will quickly find that their brain has atrophied. They will come to the surprising conclusion that, in the past year, not one single original thought has sailed through their heads.

Brits are taking much more care over their appearance than they've ever done before; it shows a certain amount of pride, as well as an ever larger slice of vanity. But do these people seriously expect to be going to the gym when they're in their 60s? A shallow number aspire to just this. They want to mix with thirtysomethings, and be mistaken for thirtysomethings. But in their quest for eternal youth, they have turned themselves into standing jokes.

Compare the stars who are obsessed with their looks to people of the same age who are keen to stay mentally agile and alert. Are they figures of fun or do we admire these people, and remark upon how amazing it is that their minds are still as quick as steel traps?

From: *The Scotsman*, 11 June 2003

## Lösungsvorschlag

### I. Questions on the text

1. In the past women wore metal rings around their necks to make them longer, put corsets around their waists to look slimmer or bound their feet to make them smaller. Today people not only wear high heels and take diet pills to appear tall and slim. They also spend huge amounts of money on improving their looks: men take drugs to make their bodies look athletic, women and men buy beauty products whose effect is at least doubtful. Some women also undergo surgery in order to enlarge their breasts so as to become more attractive.

2. In former times Puritans regarded people's preoccupation with the beauty business as frivolous and and thundered against the use of lipstick and facepaint. Today critics hold that the beauty industry cheats people out of money and also that society is in danger of becoming more and more superficial. They also think that the beauty craze today disrupts families and leads to eating disorders. Other critics are concerned that the line between cosmetics and drugs is becoming blurred or see cosmetic surgery as a first step towards genetic manipulation.

3. Athletes want to improve their performance in order to be more competitive, but the main reason for physical enhancement is still the search for beauty. This shouldn't be surprising as the promises made in advertisements have been confirmed by various studies. Attractive people tend to earn more than ugly ones, especially in sales jobs. (ll. 37–42). It goes without saying that good looks "help in the marriage market". (l. 43) Moreover, since most people, even babies, feel more attracted to good-looking people, the handsome have been shown to be better parents (l. 45) and more self-confident (l. 44, ll. 46/47). Finally, pretty people are also the first to get help when they have a problem (ll. 47/48) and even get away with milder sentences when they have committed a crime (ll. 48–50).

4. The author thinks that in the case of teenagers the parents should be held responsible for youngsters tampering with their bodies. He thinks that no one can object to straightening teeth or even noses, but when it comes to removing fat from the body, getting tattoos or even breast enlargement parents should prevent their children from doing so.
   However, if adults want to change their looks, they should be allowed to do so. The author calls it "one of the most basic human liberties" to fall for the promises of the cosmetics firms (ll. 34/35). The state should only intervene in legal matters, such as forcing the firms to list the ingredients of their beauty products on the pots or packages.

5. Both in the title and in the last paragraph the author refers to people's right to be beautiful. But whereas the headline categorically claims a "right to be beautiful", the author discusses its aspects in the last paragraph and raises the question of whether society should pay for cosmetic operations. He argues that we have successfuly abolished the differences between rich and poor in matters of health care. And he refers to the World Health Organization's broadened definition of health by pointing out that a person's outward appearance can also have a tremendous effect on his or her well-being. Thus, with cosmetic surgery being very advanced, he wonders if the public shouldn't have to pay for cosmetic surgery in order to wipe out inequalities.

6. *Note: In order to convey his message that the individuals are responsible and should consider what they do with their bodies, the author mixes serious and humorous passages. We have selected five examples, because we consider them typical of the author's tone and use of language:*

   - "What sane person would put metal rings round her neck to stretch it like a giraffe's …? How backward, how primitive. Completely different from … the woman who pays huge sums to have her breasts surgically enlarged …"(ll. 1–4)

     In his introduction the author's tone is definitely ironic: contrasting primitive practices with our allegedly sensible ones, he makes it clear that we are not really different from those peoples. His feigned indignation shows in the ellipsis: "How backward, how primitive." (l. 3)

   - "… modern men and women … spend $160 billion a year on beauty products whose impact on the appearance is sometimes, um, unproven." (ll. 5–7)

     This part finishes the praise of our "sensible" modern methods; by putting in the interjection "um" – which we use when are not quite sure about what we are saying – he reveals that his statement is ironic.

   - "…a bit of lipstick can keep you out of jail, or waxing your moustache can land an extra 15% in earnings…" (ll. 51/52)

     Having mentioned that good-looking people enjoy a number of privileges in life, he uses hyperbole, i.e. he deliberately exaggerates their advantages, thus directing an ironic pinprick at society's obsession with attractiveness and showing his critical attitude towards it.

   - "Others … complain that tampering with the incline of one's nose is the first step on a slippery slope to tampering with one's genes." (ll. 20–22)

     In this passage the author's tone is serious. He expresses his and the critics' doubts about cosmetic surgery and heightens the effect by using the metaphor and alliteration "step on a slippery slope".

   - "Until their bodies stop growing, teenagers should not be allowed to change them in permanent ways that may turn out to be harmful. By all means straighten their teeth and even their noses, but leave puppy fat alone. Let them pierce their ears … but ban the tattoos and hold that graduation present of breast enlargement." (ll. 24–28)

     The author's tone is at first very serious when he rejects cosmetic surgery on adolescents. But then he addresses the adult readers directly with an imperative to tell them about their responsibility. Here he employs some informal words (puppy fat) and chooses extreme, far-fetched examples ("hold that graduation present of breast enlargement") to illustrate his message. Thus the tone becomes humorous.

   *Note that the author also uses a lot of serious questions in order to make the reader draw his own conclusions (ll. 11/12, ll. 17/18, l. 29, ll. 56/57)*

## II. Composition

1. **"Every generation laughs at the old fashions, but follows religiously the new" (Henry David Thoreau, 1817–1862). Comment on this statement.**

   *Note: First look up in your dictionary what "religiously" means: "very carefully or regularly" (OALD). So those who follow the new fashion religiously are very careful to always wear the latest fashion craze.*

   Have you ever looked at an old photograph of yourself? You may wonder if you really looked like that and even laugh at your old trousers, skirts and your haircut. Then you may come to the conclusion that you look much better today and that the fashion ten or fifteen years ago was "impossible".

   What you do not realise, however, is that today you are just following another fashion trend, which may look equally outdated in ten years. Most of us would probably not admit that we are trying to keep up with fashion and say that we dress and style ourselves only according to our taste. But that is just the point: our tastes are formed by stylists and designers. When fashion trends are set they insidiously influence our tastes.

   Of course there are those of us who dress like our favourite film stars, who want to look like models on the catwalk and always buy the latest fashion. They do indeed follow the new fashion "religiously", i.e. they are very careful to wear what is "in" at the moment.

   But there are also some who do not care about fashion at all, who refuse to conform to the common taste. They may easily become the laughingstock of the rest of us. People tend to call them old-fashioned or even weird. That is because most of us, although we may be far from admitting it, try to keep up with fashion to a certain extent. We may not follow it "religiously", as Thoreau suggested, but we can't really avoid being influenced by it.

2. **"The surest way to corrupt a youth is to instruct him to hold in higher esteem those who think alike than those who think differently" (Friedrich Nietzsche, 1844–1900). Comment on the statement.**

   When Friedrich Nietzsche said that you corrupt a youth by teaching him to respect those who think like himself more than his opponents he certainly wanted to challenge the authorities of his time. The aphorism may also contain a sideswipe at the priests and teachers, who tried to hammer their own ideas into their pupils' heads. Being critical of any "absolute truth" and rebelling against the authorities of his time, Nietzsche saw the aim of education as educating critical people, who were prepared to question their own ideas, accept their opponents' views and who learned to think dialectically.

   Today the statement is still highly topical. Totalitarian regimes leave no doubt as to what their young people are supposed to think and tend to conceal all critical ideas from them. Or take some religious extremists in the USA: parents refuse to send their children to school because they do not want to expose them to being taught the theory of evolution. They are only allowed to learn the biblical concept that the world was created in seven days.

   How can these youths ever become free and critical thinkers?

   But that is exactly what we need – critical, well-rounded personalities, who have the ability to question the assertions and decisions of governments and other authorities and who can form their own opinions. Otherwise they can easily be manipulated and controlled by just a few powerful people in the media or in government positions. If we understand it in this way Nietzsche's statement hasn't lost its topicality.

3. **Do you really need a tattoo?**

Tattoos have become extremely popular in the last ten years, especially with young people. Once an adornment of sailors and bikers, they can now be seen on the shoulders, arms, ankles and bellies of a lot of celebrities, athletes, film stars and pop musicians. The types are just as varied as their locations: flowers, symbols, slogans, even the names of loved ones adorn their muscles. And a lot of young people just follow the fashion, thinking that it is "cool" to sport a tattoo.

If you have ever thought of getting one, too, you should think twice whether you really need one. Don't forget that tattoos are just a fashion, and that like other fashions, they change frequently. What is now considered to be "in" or sexy may look very old-fashioned and unattractive in a few years. You can easily become a figure of fun for your own children And then you mustn't forget that our tastes are subject to change. What if you do not like the motif on your skin any more in a few years? And do you really want to surprise your sweetheart with the name of his or her predecessor on your skin?

You can have a tattoo removed with special laser lights today, but it is still costly and very likely to leave a scar. Let us face the truth: tattoos are for life. If you can accept that, it is okay. But if you have any doubts whether you really want the motif on your skin for the rest of your days, you should think twice about getting one.

4. **A reporter talks to an athlete who has tested positive for illegal substances. Write up the interview published in a sports magazine.**

JOURNALIST: Mr Jones, is it true that you tested positive for modafinil – a banned stimulant – at the last national championships and have been suspended from the Olympic Games in Athens?

MR JONES: Well, all I can tell you is that I was notified that they had tested my A sample – which was positive – and would now test the B sample. We will have to wait for the results.

JOURNALIST: But Mr. Jones, you know as well as I that in 99% of the cases the B sample confirms the original positive test. So we may well ask you why you took these banned substances.

MR JONES: I have never taken any illegal substances as far as I know …

JOURNALIST: Do you really want us to believe that you are a poor victim?

MR JONES: All I'm saying is that I am not a doctor nor do I know anything about drugs and their effects. Everyone knows that I have always been a fervent advocate of a "clean" sport because I strongly believe in fair play – and taking stimulants gives you an unfair advantage …

JOURNALIST: And yet, you have tested positive …

MR JONES: I told you, we still have to wait for the B sample. And as I have tried to point out my doctors gave me medicine I had to take when I had a cold – that may have contained the substances. I do not think that they checked the doping list every time they administered cough medecine to me. So, if I really took the drug – which I still doubt – I took it unwittingly.

JOURNALIST: Mr Jones, thank you very much for the interview.

## III. Translation

Das Gehirn ist genauso ein Muskel wie jeder andere Teil des Körpers; und je mehr man es trainiert, desto kräftiger und widerstandsfähiger[1] wird es. Aber daraus folgt auch[2], dass Leute, die sich nicht ständig selbst fordern, schnell feststellen werden, dass ihr Gehirn verkümmert ist. Sie werden zu der überraschenden Schlussfolgerung gelangen, dass im vergangenen Jahr kein einziger orgineller Gedanke durch ihren Kopf gegangen[3] ist.
Die Briten achten jetzt[4] viel mehr auf ihr Aussehen als jemals zuvor; das zeigt ein gewisses Maß an Stolz sowie eine noch größere Portion Eitelkeit. Aber erwarten diese Leute im Ernst, dass sie noch ins Fitnessstudio gehen werden, wenn sie über sechzig sind? Eine geringe Zahl[5] hat sich genau dies vorgenommen. Sie wollen sich mit Leuten, die in den Dreißigern sind, zusammentun und wollen für Leute zwischen dreißig und vierzig[6] gehalten werden. Aber in ihrem Streben nach ewiger Jugend machen sie sich zu Witzfiguren[7].
Vergleichen wir die Stars, die von ihrem Aussehen besessen sind mit gleichaltrigen Leuten, die darauf aus sind, geistig regsam und wach zu bleiben. Sind Sie Witzfiguren oder bewundern wir diese Leute und geben unserem Erstaunen darüber Ausdruck[8], dass ihr Geist immer noch so schnell zuschnappt wie ein Fangeisen[9]?

Anmerkung:

1 *robuster* wird natürlich auch anerkannt
2 stilistisch bedingte Einfügung
3 wörtl. *gesegelt*
4 *jetzt* zur Wiedergabe des Aspekts – auch als Gegensatz zu *früher („before")*
5 *„a shallow number"* ist im Englischen doppeldeutig, daher ist auch die Übersetzung *Eine Anzahl oberflächlicher Leute* ... möglich.
6 möglich ist natürlich auch *in den Dreißigern*
7 *„a standing joke"* ist wörtlich *ein bewährter Witz*
8 *„and remark upon how amazing it is"* wurde zu *geben unserem Erstaunen darüber Ausdruck* zusammengefasst
9 Das Bild *Ihr Geist ist so schnell wie eine Stahlfalle* wirkt im Deutschen schief – mit dieser Version wurde versucht, eine etwas freiere Übersetzung zu wählen, die dennoch fast orginalgetreu ist. Ein adäquates Bild im Deutschen wäre auch *dass ihre Geist noch immer messerscharf ist.*

## Leistungskurs Englisch 2004
## Textaufgabe II

**Timothy Findley, *Dinner Along the Amazon***

Every morning at seven o'clock Harper Dewey turned over and woke up. And every morning he would lie in his tumbled bed (for he slept without repose even at the age of eight) until it was seven-thirty, thinking his way back into his dreams, which were always of his father. At seven-thirty he would get out of bed and cross to his window where he would stand for a moment watching his dreams fade in the sunlight until there was nothing in the garden save the lilac and the high board fence.

And the birds.

Robins and starlings and sparrows flowed over the smooth lawn in great droves, turning it into the likeness of a marketplace; and the raucous babble of their bargaining (of dealings in worms and beetles and flies) poured itself, like something distilled or dehydrated, from the jar of darkness into the morning air, which made it swell and burst. This enormous shout of birds at morning was always a delight to Harper Dewey.

Presently, over this sound, there would burst the first indication of an awakening household: Bertha Millroy's hymn.

Bertha Millroy was the maid – and a day, to Bertha, wasn't a day at all unless it began with a hymn and ended with a prayer.

She lived – Bertha – in the attic, in a small room directly above Harper's room and she sang her hymn from the window which opened over his head. When it was finished she would say the same thing every morning – "Amen" and "Good morning Harper." Then they would race each other to the landing on the stairs. Harper never cheated, although he could easily have been dressed long before Bertha if he had chosen to be, because he was always awake so much earlier than her. But this every morning race had never been specifically agreed upon and if Harper had ever said to Bertha at the window "Let's race," or if Bertha had ever said to Harper below her "Beat you downstairs," the whole procedure would have been off. Neither of them could remember when this habit had started – it just had.

Well, one morning early in the summer, (in fact it was hardly more than late spring), Harper and Bertha met on the stairs' landing – Bertha won – and after they had scanned the note they found there, they looked at each other and then quickly looked away. They descended to the first floor in their usual fashion – Harper going down the front stairs to collect the paper from the front porch – and Bertha going down the back stairs to light the stove and to bring in the milk.

This morning, Harper didn't open the paper, although he usually read the comics sitting on the porch step. Instead he returned inside, letting the screen door clap behind him and leaving the big oak and glass door open so that the air could come through, into the still house. He went straight out to the kitchen and sat down at the table, slipping the still folded paper onto the breakfast tray which was laid out for his mother.

In the kitchen, Bertha Millroy behaved in the same morose fashion, as though touched by the same hand. And indeed their mutual despondency was based upon a kindred misgiving. And Mrs Renalda Harper Dewey was the instigator of that misgiving.

Mrs Renalda Harper Dewey, widow of Harper Dewey the First (killed in the battle for Caen, August 1944, the year after Harper P. Dewey the Second's birth) was a lady who lay in bed till nine o'clock every morning because of the night before[1]. It used to be that she would lie abed until eight and then it became an occasional night before – but now the lieabed was until nine and had ceased to be occasional.

This morning there had been a note on the flat top of the balustrade on the landing. On the note were written the words "Ten o'clock – thank you" in rather indistinct watery blue ink. "Ten o'clock, thank you" and that was all.

Bertha put on the kettle.
"I don't want any tea," said Harper Dewey.
"You don't drink morning tea because you want to, Master[2] Harper Dewey," said Bertha Millroy in her flat voice, "You drink it to assist nature."
The kettle boiled.
Bertha warmed the teapot.
They were silent.
Bertha threw out the water into the sink and put tea leaves in the pot.
The robins moved across the lawn outside the kitchen window.
Harper watched them.
Bertha poured boiling water over the tea leaves, turned off the stove and put the lid on the teapot. One, two, three, and sat down.
"Ten o'clock indeed," she muttered – and then she poured tea into their cups.

One of the robins was listening to a worm under the dew. Harper watched. The robin's head was cocked to one side as it listened. Then it ran a few steps on tiptoe and caught the worm noise again – this time nearer to it. The robin waited. Harper waited – Bertha Millroy waited – and then the robin stabbed the ground with its beak – caught the worm and tossed it into the sunlight. Harper shivered.

"I don't want to assist nature," he said, and he pushed his teacup away.



1 the night before: cf. the expression "the morning after the night before", used to describe how someone feels the next morning after an occasion when they have drunk too much alcohol

2 Master: title, now old-fashioned but in the 1950s still normal, for a boy too young to be called "Mister"

**Worksheet:**

maximum number of points attainable

**I. Questions on the text**

Read all the questions first, then answer them in the given order. Use your own words as far as is appropriate.

1. Describe the social background and the present situation of the Dewey family. 10
2. Analyse the relationship between Harper and Bertha. 20
3. Characterize Bertha and Harper. 20
4. Examine the significance of the note and its effect on Harper and Bertha. What is hereby revealed about the role of the mother in the family? 20

5. How does the author create suspense? Consider the narrative perspective in your answer. 10
6. Compare the two passages about birds in this excerpt (ll. 7–12 and 57–67) and explain their function in the text. 20

## II. Composition

Choose *one* of the following topics. Write about 250 to 300 words. 50

1. Has society become too tolerant of drinking?
2. "Today you need a licence for almost everything but not for having children" was the topic of a magazine article. Write a letter to the editor outlining the qualifications you think necessary for a 'parenting licence'.
3. "Happiness is having a large, loving, caring, close-knit family in another city" (George Burns, 1896–1996). Comment on this statement.
4. "The worst solitude is to be destitute of sincere friendship" (Sir Francis Bacon, 1561–1628). Comment on this statement.

## III. Translation

Translate the following text into German: 50

200

"I don't know how to begin ...," says the narrator in the opening sentence of the story that begins Timothy Findley's career as a writer of fiction.

The openings of Findley's narratives are often linked with a loss of innocence, and in his early work this loss is often imaged through the figure of a troubled adolescent whose fall from childhood is at the core of the narrative. The early narratives circle around sexuality, mental illness, and violence, portraying them through the eyes of children. The adults in these stories engage in a conspiracy of silence about the frightening things that are happening in their families – parents who refuse to be parents, people who drink themselves into oblivion, shoot themselves, drive their cars off cliffs. From the adult point of view, these are unspeakable acts that must never enter the discourse of society. Perhaps the adults are attempting to protect the children, to keep them innocent. But the prolonged innocence is double edged. It builds up unbearable tension, generating an insatiable desire to break the silence. The stories of these families must be told – and the desire to tell them is embodied in Findley's children. Yet they don't know how to begin.

From: Anne Geddes Bailey/Karen Grandy (eds.), *Paying Attention: Critical Essays on Timothy Findley*. Toronto: ECW Press 1998

---

## Lösungsvorschlag

### I. Questions on the text

1. The family seems to be rather wealthy. The Deweys live in their own house, which is impressive enough to have a porch, a big oak and glass door (l. 35) and a garden that attracts numerous birds. They can afford the services of a maid, and even seven years after her husband's death the widow does not need to work for a living and can sleep as long as she desires. The names of the late father and his son (Harper P. Dewey the First and the Second) suggest a certain family pride and tradition.

2. Socially Harper and Bertha would be defined as young master and servant. It is obvious, however, that these two people share a considerable understanding and familiarity. They have a tradition of racing each other to the landing (l. 20) every morning, like playful friends, and of never cheating. Without words they understand each other's feelings ("they looked at each other and then quickly looked away", l. 29). They don't conceal their misgivings about Mrs Dewey's increasing alcoholism from each other ("I don't want any tea", l. 50; "Ten o'clock indeed", l. 61). Betty behaves confidently towards "Master" Harper – she criticises him for refusing his tea and seems to have an important role in his upbringing ("You don't drink morning tea because you want to", l. 51 ).

3. Bertha Millroy is openly religious, controlled and reliable. She routinely begins her day by singing hymns from her window before she diligently assumes her tasks of keeping house and looking after the eight-year-old in a competent way. It can be seen by her concern about Mrs Dewey's weakness that she feels responsible for the family's well-being.
   Harper, untypical of a small boy, is a restless sleeper. His dreams are about his father – even though he didn't really know him – because he feels, subconsciously, that things would not be as bleak if he was still around. Even so Harper is always delighted by the song of the birds in the garden. He keeps up a certain stability by observing his daily routines, is too honest to ever cheat Bertha at their race, and shows sensitivity in grasping the implication of his mother's note.

4. *Note: The question requires three comments: about the significance of the note, its effect, and his mother's role.*

   The note reveals to Betty and Harper that Mrs Dewey has changed for the worse. She used to sleep until eight o'clock, then started the habit of drinking the night before and slept until nine, but now for the first time she feels unable to rise before ten.
   The effect on the other members of the household is one of consternation. They look at each other quickly and instantly realize what the note means. It makes them morose and despondent (l. 38 f). Harper neither feels like reading the comics nor having his tea as usual. In the kitchen they remain hushed, only Bertha expresses her discontent (l. 61).
   Mrs Dewey's absence in this text is telling. She is no part of the family in the morning and, by letting herself go, cannot assume her role as mother of a fatherless son and lady of the house. Instead of talking things over she leaves notes and worries the others ("the instigator of that misgiving", l. 40).

5. The author uses the perspective of the third-person narrator who, from his unlimited view, can decide how much he wants to reveal and when to do so.
   He casually lets Harper and Betty find the note whose content remains mysterious. The reader can only infer from the characters' reactions that a problem is at hand. So one is

kept in suspense until later on when the author decides to disclose the circumstances and the message.

6. In the first passage Harper watches different birds flying about joyfully and in great numbers. It seems like a scene from a lively marketplace where worms and insects are traded. Their singing makes Harper happy, their unfailing presence every morning is part of his schedule and conveys an element of security.
   In the second passage, however, the variety of birds has narrowed down to robins and particularly to one single bird which stalks a worm, catches it and throws it up into the air, to the dismay of the two watchers. Here the bird is no part of an idyllic setup anymore, but is shown as a predator that kills his victim.
   The gleeful presence and happy noises of the birds in the first passage underline Harpers cheerfulness. The second passage comes after the discovery of the note, when his mood has darkened. The bird's tossing up the worm into the sunlight parallels the realization of his mother's deterioration, and Harper does not "want to assist nature" (l. 67) anymore.

## II. Composition

1. **Has society become too tolerant of drinking?**

   Alcohol has become omnipresent. Magazines and TV commercials try to induce people to drink certain brands, film characters can hardly get by without the help of whiskeys or martinis. Campaigns against smoking are gaining in intensity while hardly anybody raises their voice against liquor. Have we become too tolerant of drinking?
   Nobody can deny that alcohol is as detrimental to people's health as tobacco, and yet it has turned into a widespread addiction. Doctors and politicians occasionally warn against excessive drinking, especially where children are concerned. There are laws which – rather unsuccessfully – try to make it impossible for minors to have access to alcoholic drinks. In Germany the government has just agreed to raise the tax on so-called alco-pops, in which the alcohol is hidden in a fruity and sweet liquid, to discourage teenagers from buying their favourite party drink. But there has been no vigorous attempt to make adults cut down on their liquor as well. Drinking is responsible for too many road accidents, for wife battering, broken homes and freakish behaviour. Yet it still seems to be socially acceptable. Hosts may be quite categorical in discouraging their guests from smoking but no party is conceivable without beer, wine or spirits. People drink their inhibitions and problems away and habitually feel good about it. Criticising drinking would rather be like criticising oneself – who would want to start a discussion about the drug alcohol if one seems to need it so much? It is sad to say, but we do have too much tolerance of drinking.

2. **Write a letter to the editor outlining the qualifications you think necessary for a "parenting licence".**

   *Note: The following essay is written in an ironic tone*

   Dear Sir or Madam,

   I was intrigued by your article about a licence for parents, in your latest edition, and would like to enter the discussion you initiated.
   Let us put aside the unfortunate fact that without due consideration you can automatically become a parent by giving birth to a child or fathering one.
   But if there were a parenting licence it would have to be granted under the following conditions:
   - Prior to applications candidates have to pass tests in baby-care and youth psychology with a grade average of no less than 70 %

- To qualify as a parent applicants have to be at least 25 years of age to warrant a certain probability of maturity and responsibility
- To provide for the child's sustenance applicants for the licence have to demonstrate a regular disposable income of no less than £20 000 per annum
- Singles or homosexuals need not apply as only normal families offer the necessary background for a baby's sound and safe development
- Candidates have to prove their aptitude for parenthood by submitting a declaration of two pages (minimum) explaining why they should be eligible for a parenting licence
- Affidavits[1] from the applicant's employer and a social worker are imperative
- If there is any change in circumstances the licence may be withdrawn at any time

With the acceptance of the stipulations above we would finally be able to close a painful gap in our otherwise monolithic structure of regulations, wouldn't we?

Yours tongue-in-cheek

Betty Harper

1 beglaubigte oder eidesstattliche Erklärung

3. **"Happiness is having a large, loving, caring, close-knit family in another city". Comment on this statement.**

George Burns, who lived to the biblical age of 100, surely had a rich treasure of experience and worldly wisdom at his command. His longevity would not have been possible had he not led a happy life, and we are advised not to take his aphorism lightly. Though having a large family has gone out of fashion nobody would complain if one's family was a loving and caring one, and a close-knit one to boot.
What makes the quotation so piquant is its anticlimax – this happy family should ideally live in another city to make the father and husband truly happy, too (As in the case of Mr Burns, who was born two centuries ago and must have been a stolid patriarch – thus we can neglect the concept of a wife and mother enjoying the same distance to her family). So what was Mr Burns likely to be up to when he removed himself geographically from his loved ones? Obviously he cherished the freedom to pursue pastimes and habits that would have been frowned upon by his wife and children, like keeping and entertaining a mistress or two, frequenting night clubs or inviting raucous friends over and drinking at his pleasure, polluting the environment with the smoke of his cigars, and generally making a mess of his room.
Without these beneficial liberties no doubt Mr Burns' happiness would have been much reduced, but by living in two worlds he could combine the advantages of both and be wonderfully happy ever after. I only have the suspicion that nowadays it might be rather difficult to be blessed with a family of such consenting dispositions.

4. **"The worst solitude is to be destitute of sincere friendship". Comment on this statement.**

*Note: In this case it is worth looking up "solitude" in your dictionary: when you are alone, especially when this is what you enjoy (DCE). It also refers you to "loneliness" (unhappy because you are alone), and gives you related words like lonesome, solitary, even lone wolf – if you can use it!*

It may well be that in Sir Francis Bacon's time the word solitude had a different ring to it. Nowadays it rather means being alone and enjoying it (DCE), so that the 'worst' solitude doesn't seem to make much sense and is a contradiction in terms. Bacon's age, however, the age of absolutism, was also full of contradictions. One of his contemporaries, King Eugene of Württemberg, had a splendid castle built for himself in the woods which he named 'Solitude', and regularly invited a host of courtiers and companions to hunt and make merry with him. It is quite possible that among his followers he didn't have one sincere friend and wouldn't have been aware of the deficiencies of 'solitude' according to Bacon.

The quotation comes alive if we define solitude as loneliness, which is a solitude nobody enjoys, which means being alone and friendless. Thus loneliness would be sad enough if one had nobody or just friends, in the superficial sense of the word, to spend time and share one's thoughts with. What makes this loneliness the 'worst solitude', however, is when you realize the absence of 'sincere' friends. Those are not just people that are around when you need company but people you can trust completely, who are honest with you and stand by you in distress. If you don't have any of those you can feel alone even in company.

You are to be pitied because it makes you aware of having fallen into the worst solitude imaginable.

## III. Translation

„Ich weiß nicht, wie ich anfangen soll …", sagt der Erzähler im ersten Satz der Geschichte, mit der Timothy Findleys literarische Karriere[1] beginnt. Die Anfänge von Findleys Erzählungen stehen oft in Zusammenhang mit einem Verlust der Unschuld, und in seinem Frühwerk wird dieser Verlust oft durch die Person eines problembeladenen Jugendlichen verkörpert, dessen plötzlicher Abschied von seiner Kindheit den Kern der Geschichte bildet. Die frühen Erzählungen kreisen um die Themen[2] Sexualität, geistige Verwirrung und Gewalt, die aus der Sicht von Kindern geschildert werden. Die Erwachsenen in diesen Geschichten decken den Mantel des Stillschweigens [3] über die fürchterlichen Dinge, die in ihren Familien geschehen – Eltern, die sich weigern Eltern zu sein, Leute, die sich bis zur Besinnungslosigkeit[4] betrinken, die sich erschießen, die sich mit ihren Autos von Klippen stürzen. Aus erwachsener Sicht sind dies unaussprechliche Handlungen, die niemals in der Gesellschaft thematisiert[5] werden dürfen. Vielleicht versuchen die Erwachsenen auch[2], die Kinder zu schützen, ihnen ihre Unschuld zu bewahren. Aber die künstlich verlängerte Zeit[6] der Unschuld ist zweischneidig. Sie baut eine unerträgliche Spannung auf, die ein unstillbares Verlangen erzeugt, das Schweigen zu brechen. Die Geschichten dieser Familien müssen einfach[2] erzählt werden – und der Drang sie zu erzählen ist in Findleys Kindern verkörpert. Und doch wissen sie nicht, wie sie anfangen sollen.

Anmerkungen

1 *Literarisch* bedeutet im Deutschen vorwiegend belletristisch – *'writer of fiction'* mit *‚Autor schöngeistiger Literatur'* zu übersetzen wäre übertrieben. Möglich wäre auch *Prosaschriftsteller*

2 Stilistisch bedingte Einfügungen

3 wörtlich: *gehen eine Verschwörung des Schweigens ein*

4 *oblivion* wörtlich: *das Vergessen*

5 *discourse* – hier: eine Rede oder ein Gespräch ernsten Inhalts

6 *künstlich* und *Zeit* sind Einfügungen, welche die Aussage verdeutlichen

## Leistungskurs Englisch 2005
## Textaufgabe I

### Voting's too good for 'em

Politics is a curious business. Democracy is sacred and we go to war to bring its beneficence to benighted peoples. We celebrate as every decade it spreads further across a globe where now a majority of humans live under its benign glow.

How odd then that democracy's high priests and priestesses, the politicians, are treated with almost universal contempt. Democracy is holy, politics is lowly. 'The people' are noble, while those they elect are contemptible.

But sometimes when you go out there on the street to watch democracy in action, the nobility of 'the people' is a lot less striking than the patience and tolerance of their servants, the politicians. It is salutary to be reminded how much sheer pig-headed ignorance, nastiness, mean-spiritedness and rudeness politicians encounter every day. Trying to squeeze votes out of people who can't be bothered to inform themselves of the most basic facts is wearying work. "Don't care, never vote, you're all the same, just in it for yourselves, what's in it for me and when are you going to fix my drainpipe?" Faced with some of that grudge, ordinary mortals might give 'the people' a stinging earful, but of course no politician dare.

Calling Labour HQ to find who (if anyone) was out pressing the flesh for next week's Euro elections[1], I was offered Jack Straw[2] on a swing[3] around Canterbury, Deal, Broadstairs and Ramsgate. It was not a red-carpet outing – the train offering just one sandwich and no water for him and his hungry entourage.

Out there at one end of Deal high street a flotilla of Labour grandees was waiting; cheering them up is the main success of this otherwise fairly unfruitful expedition. In this constituency with a 5,000 Labour majority, working our way down the main street, what do we find? It's an odd business, approaching total strangers with a jovial handshake, the sort of behaviour that marks out politicians as abnormal beings.

Outside Marks & Spencer[4], Straw stands on a milk crate to give a rousing hymn of praise for all that Europe has done for Deal. Today he tells how, since D-day, the EU has brought peace and prosperity to all, how it is the engine of democracy from Spain to Estonia. See how its free trade delivers jobs? Remember how air travel cost an arm and a leg? Thank the EU for cheap fares, freeing up competition. "Don't let the Tories throw it away!"

So what does he get back from this desultory crowd? "You stand there talking about all the wonderful things in Europe, but when are you going to do something for us here at home?" Daft, irrelevant, or what? The man is indignant that he gets less benefit because he's got £16,000 in the bank. Next up, an angry man: "Why am I paying £77 a month council tax, worked all my life and got nothing for it?" Because it's a Tory council that put it up 9.7 % this year, but he's still going to vote Tory anyway. "Why isn't the police station here open full time?" calls the next man. Not one voice takes up the European theme.

Local MP Gwyn Prosser works the crowd, picking up complaints. "Why hasn't the council fixed my fence?" says a man who claims he always voted Labour, but now he's going to vote BNP[5]. Why? "Well, Europe. I don't agree with one big state, not at all. England for the English." His MP takes him on: "Vote for that xenophobic, fascist party?" Turns out he's a liar. Labour records show he never voted at all last time and he has never been

Labour. But the people are always right, free to lie through their teeth, unlike their leaders.

Next man up tells me: "They give asylum seekers £160 a week for a single bloke." No, they don't, says the MP, but no one believes him. Prod them a bit and most here are anti-European. 'Europe' has become a euphemism for 'asylum', as Michael Howard[6] well knows, blending the two together wickedly. In vain, the MP quotes latest asylum figures: a year ago 70 a day claimed asylum in Dover, now it is less than seven. But no one believes figures, they just know. Except they don't. In a haze, many confuse the EU constitution and the euro.

That's a day in the life of democracy, not much sublime and a lot of ridiculous. A busy foreign secretary in the middle of a war goes out to listen to complaints about fences and persuade the wretchedly indifferent to vote pro-European. Politicians are the people who do democracy, day in, day out. And day in, day out they are kicked in the teeth for it. Too often we commentators sit in lofty judgement. But we are accountable to no one, just perusing polls, while they have to navigate seas of actual voters who may make scant sense, who vote on whim or through habit.

Politicians are despised partly for their virtues – their willingness to listen and explain anything to anyone, however rude. But often voters deserve a good wigging[7]. What about the democratic responsibilities that go with rights? Ask not what your country can do for you … Stop whingeing, start thinking. Get informed. Make an effort. The country's future is in your hands, not politicians'. At least get out there and goddamn vote, which quite a few said they wouldn't. One small step towards making citizens take democracy more seriously would be to oblige them all to vote.

From an article by Polly Toynbee in: *The Guardian*, 4 June 2004

1 Euro elections: the elections to the European Parliament in June 2004
2 Jack Straw: the Foreign Secretary
3 swing: a journey with quick stops
4 Marks & Spencer: British department store
5 BNP: British National Party
6 Michael Howard: leader of the Conservative Party
7 wigging: scolding

**Worksheet:**

maximum number of points attainable

## I. Questions on the text

Read all the questions first, then answer them in the given order. Use your own words as far as is appropriate.

1. "Democracy is holy, politics is lowly." (l. 5). Explain the meaning of this sentence. — 10
2. Examine the picture the writer paints of politicians. — 20
3. What arguments does Straw give to underline the importance of Europe and what do voters actually think about Europe? — 20
4. Outline the voters' behaviour and interests as depicted in the text. — 20
5. Considering the writer's intention, analyse the language and the tone of the text. — 20
6. Analyse the meaning of the title. — 10

## II. Composition

Choose *one* of the following topics. Write about 250 to 300 words. 50

1. "Ask not what your country can do for you – ask what you can do for your country." (John F. Kennedy) Discuss.
2. "Democracy is a device that ensures we shall be governed no better than we deserve." (George Bernard Shaw) Discuss.
3. Europe – a promising concept? Discuss.
4. Write a letter to your representative in the European Parliament telling him/her about the issue(s) worrying you and your generation. Suggest possible solutions.

## III. Translation

Translate the following text into German: 50

200

Falling turnout is a trend visible all over the world. During the European elections in Britain in 1999, fewer than half the electorate voted. Even in eastern European countries that became democracies as recently as 1989–91, turnout has been falling. People don't turn out to vote, not because they already know who will win, but because they don't believe that politicians can or will deliver.

Nor are people ignoring the ballot box because the process of voting is too old-fashioned. It's true that the trudge to the voting station, the oversized slip of paper to be crossed with a pencil, is ill fitting with the techno-friendly Britain of the twenty-first century.

It's true also that internet or telephone voting, or an extended ballot period, might beef up the turnout. One million people voted via the internet and a freephone number to change Kellogg's *Choco Krispies* brand name back to *Coco Pops* after all. But the problem isn't ultimately one of accessibility; it is one of disillusionment. People are not voting because they have just stopped believing that politics matters.

Politics has become a product not really worth buying, another offer battling for the consumers' attention via ever more slick[1] advertising campaigns rather than substance.

From *It's not about apathy* by Noreena Hertz in:
*The Observer*, 10 June 2001

Anmerkung
1 slick (here): dt. raffiniert

## Lösungsvorschlag

### I. Questions on the text

1. *To answer this question you have to study lines 1–6 carefully, where Polly Toynbee deals with the subject. Be aware, however, that she uses irony in these lines.*

   On the one hand people in Britain and the western world regard the idea of democracy as 'holy' (l. 5) or 'sacred' (l. 1), as a 'benign' (i. e. good and beneficial; l. 3) system that keeps spreading in the world and contributes to the well-being of 'benighted' (i. e. primitive; l. 2) peoples.
   On the other hand, politics, the daily political business, is regarded as 'lowly' (l. 5) or contemptible (l. 6) by most people. Consequently, politicians, the policy makers, are often despised rather than revered.

2. The writer says that politicians do a much better job than the public's prejudice presumes. Accompanying Foreign Secretary Jack Straw on a tour during the European elections she reports that he and his helpers have to be content with just one sandwich while at the same time they have to work hard cheering up local politicians, shaking the hands of total strangers, giving speeches standing on a milk crate and listening to people's – often ridiculous – complaints.
   No matter how much they are criticised, even despised, politicians always try to remain patient, tolerant, friendly and polite because they know they depend on the people's votes. It seems that these virtues, even in the face of rudeness from the voters, contribute to the bad image of the politicians.

3. *The first part of the question, i. e., the arguments in favour of the EU, is dealt with in the sixth paragraph (ll. 25–30). What the voters really think of Europe is reported in the following paragraphs (ll. 32–52).*
   *Take care to distinguish between the second part of this question and Question 4!*

   According to Straw the EU has brought peace and prosperity to Europe, it has spread democracy in formerly authoritarian or even Communist countries, from the Iberian peninsula to the Baltic states. Free trade within the union has increased competition and thus created jobs and lowered prices.
   The voters presented in this text hardly care about Europe at all and are mostly interested in politics on a local level. If they think of the EU it is associated with negative feelings. They blame it – wrongly – for the number of asylum seekers as well as for the large sums of money that these people presumably get. Many voters are ill-informed and don't even know the difference between the euro and the European constitution.

4. When the voters are first mentioned in the third paragraph they are depicted as ignorant, stubborn and rude people, who lump politicians of every creed and kind together.
   After Jack Straw's speech they corroborate those judgements – not only are they ignorant about Europe, they are not even interested in it and do not listen to arguments. All they care about is local politics and their own well-being. They turn out to be selfish and want politicians to solve their personal problems.
   Although they expect politicians to be honest, they themselves do not shrink from lying. They complain about the number of asylum seekers and the benefits they allegedly receive, and when Straw tells them they are mistaken and proves his point with figures they do not believe him. They do not try to inform themselves but are happy cherishing their own prejudices. They do not really care, so it is no wonder a large number of them will abstain from voting.

5. *Note that the text abounds in stylistic devices. When analyzing the language you cannot deal with them in detail but only in so far as they affect the tone of the article. In any case, you have to begin with the writer's intention.*

   The writer deals with the subject of voter apathy and falling turnout from a different and rather unusual angle: contrary to what the public thinks, she shows that it is not the politicians who are responsible for these problems but that it is the ignorance and apathy of the voters.
   To put her message across she uses a number of stylistic devices and tones. In the first paragraph she praises the concept of democracy in exaggerated metaphorical and elevated language: "… bring its beneficence to benighted peoples", (l. 2) and "benign glow" (l. 3). In lines 4–6 she uses some antitheses (holy-lowly; noble-contemptible) to illustrate the popular prejudice. The tone here is slightly ironic.
   This contrasts strikingly with the reality she describes in the following paragraphs. She first points out in an enumeration how pig-headed, ignorant, nasty, mean-spirited and rude the voters are (ll. 9/10) and angrily states that they really deserve to be told off.
   When she comments on the voters' stupidity and hypocrisy in elliptical remarks the tone is mocking, sometimes sneering (e. g. the case in line 33: "Daft, irrelevant or what?") and contemptuous: "Turns out he's a liar." (ll. 42/43) or ironic, even sarcastic, as in lines 44/45: "But the people are always right, free to lie through their teeth …".
   In the last paragraph, however, she recovers a serious tone, when she addresses the voters directly and appeals to them: "Stop whingeing, start thinking. Get informed. Make an effort. The country's future is in your hands …" (ll. 63/64). The tone becomes even angry when she puts in some colloquialisms: "At least get out there and goddam vote …" (l. 64).

6. *When first reading the title, the reader does not know who " 'em" refers to – only when you've read the article do you know that it refers to the voters.*

   When first reading the title you do not really know to whom it refers. It is worded in colloquial language (Voting's; 'em), so it might be the people speaking. It might reflect the common prejudice that all politicians do a bad job and that it is not worth voting for any of them – it "is too good for 'em". However, the reader is made curious because he/she is at a loss as to the real meaning.
   When we read the article, however, we realise that the headline really has a different meaning. Polly Toynbee does not blame the politicians but the voters, who in her eyes are so self-centered, ignorant, uninterested, stubborn and rude that they do not deserve the right to vote. In the light of the article voting is too good for such people.

## II. Composition

1. **"Ask not what your country can do for you – ask what you can do for your country." (John F. Kennedy) Discuss.**

   Ever since President Kennedy said those famous words in his inaugural address in 1961, they have either been praised as a motto we should all adopt or criticised as a dangerous guideline.
   Those who are critical of Kennedy's aphorism think that it can be easily misused by dictatorial regimes. To them the quotation sounds eerily similar to the Nazi slogans of "You are nothing, your people is everything" or "Public need before private greed" (Gemeinnutz geht vor Eigennutz), with which they made people comply with their murderous policies. Others think that the slogan runs counter to the American dream, which encourages people to strive for their own personal advancement and financial success and thus contribute to the well-being of the US.

Kennedy, however, meant this differently. Instead of celebrating his victory in his inaugural address he appealed to his compatriots to give up their complacency and apathy and instead join him in his effort to fight tyranny, poverty, disease, and war on earth. He called upon the people of his generation to struggle to make the world a better, safer and less dangerous place to live in. In his speech he explicitly said that he didn't call upon the people to bear arms but to contribute to the rule of law in the world. Most people expect the state and the politicians to guarantee their rights, their security and well-being. Kennedy, however, wanted to remind them that it is not the task of the few on top but of each and everyone of us – including the politicians – to get involved and make the world the place we want it to be. In this sense I wholeheartedly agree with Kennedy's words and consider them still topical.

2. **"Democracy is a device that ensures we shall be governed no better than we deserve." (George Bernard Shaw) Discuss.**

   An increasing number of people in the western world do not vote at elections any more. They either say that their vote doesn't make any difference or they regard all politicians with contempt because they think they are corrupt and just want to be elected to fill their own pockets. Very often those people are the same who later complain that the government does not address their grievances. They feel that they deserve a better administration.

   What these people fail to see is that they themselves are responsible if the composition of the government does not correspond to the wishes of the majority. Let's take the United States as a case in point. In the historic Presidential election of 2004 approximately 60 % of those entitled to vote went to the ballot box. That means that roughly 40 % abstained. However, if you talk to people in America today, a lot of them say that they did not vote for the present administration. Some of them even doubt its legitimacy because the government does not have a majority of citizens behind it. It was only elected by 51 % out of the 60 % that bothered to vote.

   What these people do not understand are the rules of a democratic state. If they vote they may not be able to change very much; however, if they do not vote they will possibly get a government they did not want but which they definitely deserve. To put it in the words of Robert Kennedy: "Few will have the greatness to bend history ..., but each of us can work to change a small portion ...". If all the non-voters remembered those words and went to the next elections they would also be governed as they deserve: by a government of their choice.

3. **Europe – a promising concept? Discuss.**

   Europe's politicians hardly ever tire of singing the praises of the European project: the ever-deeper and ever-wider unification of our continent has brought us an unprecedented era of peace in this formerly warlike part of the world. It has transformed authoritarian states like Portugal and Spain as well as the communist countries of East Europe into democracies; through free trade among the member states it has contributed to affluence and prosperity in even the remotest corners of the EU

   Although all this is true, most citizens can't really be bothered by Europe. They see it as a bureaucratic monster, far away, somewhere in Brussels, which does not affect them. Others have become increasingly critical of Europe: in the Iraq crisis in 2002 it did not speak with one voice; the euro is supposed to have caused inflation, poor economic performance and unemployment. And then there is a widespread fear of never-ending enlargements, which give millions of new citizens the right to live and work in the old member states and take the already scarce jobs. They are uneasy about Europe being already too big and about decisions being made over their heads. It is now more than likely that the new European constitution will be rejected by the French and Dutch later this month.

So the European project seems to be in danger – its structures are inefficient for a union of 25 but the constitution that tries to remedy this is not likely to be ratified. Does that mean that the project is bound to fail? I refuse to think so; in my view the politicians should reopen negotiations as soon as possible but tell the people where they are heading. Where does Europe end? Do we want to accept an endless number of new members or stabilise the existing union and make it a serious partner in world affairs? If we answer these questions to the satisfaction of the people Europe can still be a promising concept.

4. **Write a letter to your representative in the European Parliament telling him/her about the issues worrying you and your generation. Suggest possible solutions.**

*Keep in mind: A letter to an MEP*[1] *should begin with "Dear Sir" (or his/her name) and end with "Yours sincerely, ..." The way the subject is worded you have to write a letter of complaint. Tell the MEP how you are affected by the issues that worry you and what you suggest to overcome the problem. Remember that your tone should be polite but firm. You may write about matters that concern the European Parliament like, e. g., too liberal genetically modified food guidelines or hygiene standards in the EU. We decided to write about the problems connected with the eastern expansion of the EU as that is more likely to worry young people at the moment.*

Dear Mr Meyer,

let me first introduce myself: my name is Felix Schmidt and I am taking the Bavarian Abitur examination at the moment. I've got reasonable marks in most subjects and would like to study engineering when I've finished school.
That is exactly why I am writing to you. When the EU was enlarged in May 2004 all the politicians told us of the enormous opportunities which the step would offer. But what we – especially the young people – have experienced so far is that it has become increasingly difficult to get a job.
You as a member of the European Parliament are no doubt aware that more and more low-wage workers come across the borders and take our jobs away. The deregulation of service industries in Europe – which you voted for – has further aggravated the problem. But what worries me and most of my schoolfellows most is that a lot of German and international companies have now begun to outsource their research and development departments to eastern Europe, where taxes are less than half as high as in western Europe. If this development goes on, it will dramatically reduce the number of jobs for engineers in Germany. That is the more annoying as we are supporting those new member states with our contributions and thus indirectly subsidising the export of our working places.
Dear Mr Meyer, as a citizen of your constituency I urge you to do everything in your power to harmonize taxes and wages in Europe – for a start no member state should be allowed to lower its corporate taxes to 19 % or even less in order to attract new businesses. If you and your colleagues in the European Parliament do not immediately address these questions, the anger and frustation with the EU in my generation will increase and endanger the whole European project.
Yours sincerely,
*Felix Schmidt*

Anmerkung
1 Member of the European Parliament

## III. Translation

Der Rückgang der Wahlbeteiligung ist ein Trend, den man in der ganzen Welt beobachten kann. Während der Europawahlen in Großbritannien 1999 gingen weniger als die Hälfte der Wahlberechtigten[1] zur Wahl. Sogar in den osteuropäischen Ländern, die erst in den Jahren[2] 1989–91 Demokratien wurden, ist die Wahlbeteiligung zurückgegangen. Die Menschen gehen nicht zur Wahl, nicht weil sie bereits wissen, wer gewinnen wird, sondern weil sie nicht glauben, dass die Politiker etwas bewirken[3] können oder wollen.
Die Leute bleiben der Wahlurne auch nicht etwa deshalb[2] fern, weil der Wahlvorgang zu altmodisch ist. Es stimmt zwar[2], dass der mühsame Gang zum Wahllokal und[2] der überdimensionale Bogen Papier, den man mit einem Bleistift ankreuzen muss, schlecht zum Technologie-freundlichen Großbritannien des einundzwanzigsten Jahrhunderts passen.
Und[2] es stimmt auch, dass Wahlen per Internet oder Telefon sowie eine längere Öffnungszeit der Wahllokale für eine höhere Wahlbeteiligung sorgen könnten. Schließlich[4] haben eine Million Menschen über das Internet und eine gebührenfreie Telefonnummer darüber abgestimmt, Kellogs Markennamen *Choco Krispies* wieder in *Coco Pops* umzubenennen. Aber das Problem ist letztlich nicht, ob man leichteren Zugang zu den Wahlen[5] hat, sondern dass man ernüchtert[6] ist. Die Leute wählen nicht, weil sie einfach nicht mehr daran glauben, dass Politik wichtig ist.
Die Politik ist zu einer Ware geworden, die es sich nicht wirklich zu kaufen lohnt, sie ist ein weiteres Angebot, das mit immer raffinierteren Werbekampagnen anstatt mit Inhalten um die Gunst der Käufer buhlt[7].

Anmerkungen

1 electorate = die Wahlbevölkerung, sollte man im Deutschen mit Wahlberechtigte wiedergeben
2 Zusätze zur Verdeutlichung
3 Alternative: „ihre (Wahl)versprechen einhalten“
4 Es ist nicht eindeutig, ob sich „after all“ (schließlich, immerhin) auf den gesamten Satz oder nur auf den zweiten Teil bezieht („doch wieder … umzubenennen“)
5 Zusatz zur Erläuterung – „eine Frage der Zugänglichkeit“ wäre im Deutschen zu vage
6 Ein Beispiel für den Austausch der Wortart: statt des englischen Nomens (disillusionment) sollte man im Deutschen ein Adjektiv (ernüchtert, enttäuscht) verwenden
7 wörtlichere Übersetzung: „… um die Aufmerksamkeit der Verbraucher ringt.“

## Leistungskurs Englisch 2005
## Textaufgabe II

At the other end of the dormitory Stuart Barry sat up in bed, talking to James Wheatley. George Turner went to join them. Stuart and George, James's gang. Stuart: tall, blond, blandly handsome, limited. Very much a follower. George: huge, big boned, coarse featured, a lump of dark hair on a bullet head. Too stupid to be a leader.

And James himself: small, wiry, a clever, impish face, and shrewd, spiteful eyes. Eyes that now seemed to be roaming, slowly and deliberately, over the dormitory.

*don't make eye contact*

Jonathan dropped his eyes and pretended to read his book, feeling himself tense, wondering what amusements James and his minions might be planning for that night, and whether he would be an unwilling party to them.

He remembered a night three weeks ago when James had decided that William Abbott had insulted him. They had waited until lights out to drag William from his bed, force him into a laundry basket, fasten its lid and send it hurtling down the fire escape so that William ended up in the sanatorium for three days with bruised ribs.

Neil Archer, one of the prefects, had come storming into the dormitory, demanding to know who was responsible, reminding them that bullying was against the rules and threatening them all with a week of early morning runs unless the guilty ones confessed.

But James and his friends had said nothing. And the rest of them remained silent, too, condemning themselves to a week of rising before dawn and running across muddy fields for an hour before breakfast. They had sat in silence because they could not do otherwise.

Because the only rule at Kirkston Abbey that really mattered was the unwritten one that you never told tales. No matter who did what to you, you never, ever told tales.

The door of the dormitory opened. Brian Harrington appeared. Brian, big and imposing, Captain of the House Rugby team. And now with the additional authority that came with being Head of House. An authority that had belonged to Paul Ellerson until …

But he didn't want to think about that.

Brian's eyes scanned the dormitory, watching as those who were not already in their beds now scurried towards them. 'Right, good night, everyone.' 'Good night, Harrington,' they chorused in response. Brian flicked off the light switch and pulled the thick, wooden door closed behind him. Leaving them alone, with the darkness and each other.

At first, silence, save for the wind that battered the windows, blowing in from the sea.

Then slowly the darkness began to fill with a soft buzzing sound; whispered conversations, hissed in voices that feared detection and punishment. Jonathan, silent himself, strained to catch James Wheatley's voice, trying to gauge his intentions, eventually detecting its high, sharp timbre, focusing in on it anxiously, only to hear James yawning and saying 'good night' to Stuart. He felt himself relax. There would be not trouble that night.

He lay on his side, curled up in a ball, listening to the other voices die away as their owners drifted down into sleep. Coughs, sniffs, sneezes, the break of bed springs as someone tried to get comfortable for the night. The occasional churning of the hot water pipe that ran along the wall. A crowded, claustrophobic black.

Thoughts of Paul Ellerson kept coming into his head. He tried to block them out, tried to think of something else. Anything else.

He thought of how much he hated the dormitory, hated the lack of privacy, hated the constant sense of being watched. He wished he had a room of his own like they had in Abbey House. Single rooms. Rooms with locks. Locks that could keep out people like James Wheatley and George Turner. Locks that allowed you to sleep easily without wondering what surprise the night might bring. He wished he was in Abbey House. Richard Rokeby was in Abbey House.

He rolled on to his Back and stared up at the ceiling, remembering the events of the morning's Latin lesson. He thought back to how Richard had spoken to Mr Ackerley. He thought of how Richard had snubbed James Wheatley. He thought of how, unbidden, Richard had come to his aid.

And as the thought of it a strange new idea took root in his head. The idea of a friendship between the two of them.

Why not? The fact that Richard had snubbed him after the lesson didn't have to mean anything. He was in a hurry. That was all.

He began to plan in his head. Tomorrow he would start up a conversation with Richard. He would try to draw him out, try to find out something about him. Find a common ground between the two of them; a foundation on which he could build.

But as he planned he came to sees the basic flaw in his reasoning. Richard wasn't like him. Richard didn't need friends. He was strong. All he needed was himself.

The idea vanished as quickly as it had come, pierced by the cold lance of logic, leaving nothing but a sense of emptiness and a small, aching desire.

*I want to be like that. Oh god, I'd give anything just to be like that.*

He lay on his back, staring up at the darkness, listening to the wind and the heavy silence that surrounded him and dreaming of being far, far away.

From: Patrick Redmond, *The Wishing Game*. London: Hodder & Stoughton 1999

**Worksheet:**

maximum number of points attainable

## I. Questions on the text

Read all the questions first, then answer them in the given order. Use your own words as far as is appropriate.

1. What does this excerpt show the reader about the education offered at Kirkston Abbey and the organisation of daily life there? — 20
2. Characterise James Wheatley and examine the role and the extent of bullying at Kirkston Abbey. — 20
3. Analyse the reaction to bullying at Kirkston Abbey. — 10
4. Characterise Jonathan and analyse his attitude towards Richard Rokeby. — 20
5. Show how the author makes use of narrative perspective and sounds in order to create atmosphere and suspense. — 30

## II. Composition

Choose *one* of the following topics. Write about 250 to 300 words. 50

1. "I would rather be a coward than brave because people hurt you when you are brave." (E. M. Forster) Discuss.
2. "Without friends no one would choose to live though he had all other goods." (Aristotle) What do you think?
3. Violence at schools has increased over the last few years. Write an article for a quality newspaper in which you analyse the causes and effects of this development.
4. You have been chosen as a spokesperson of a team which has prepared an interview with the minister of Education. Your topic is: "To what extent does school prepare us for life? Your questions can be direct questions or suggestions. Write up the interview.

## III. Translation

Translate the following text into German: 50

200

Oliver Letwin's[1] claim that he would rather beg than send his children to a local comprehensive caused such outrage that he was forced to apologise a few days later. Yet all he did was say in public what most of his social class not only thinks, but says freely in private and, of course, acts on. There are very few people who could comfortably afford to have their children privately educated but choose not to.

Sadly, many people who cannot afford to give their children the peculiar experience that is private schooling have been led to share the middle classes' unshakeable belief that this experience is intellectually superior. But the league tables[2] where top public schools always come first are misleading: these schools ruthlessly weed out "under-performers" before exams – a fact forgotten by those who think they are not only better, but kinder than state schools.

However, the benefits most parents seek from private education are less academic than social. Most parents paying school fees are not, in reality, buying a richer intellectual experience for their child but a social environment they feel comfortable with, and the prospect of future social status for their offspring.

From *Going private, the alibi* by Judith Williamson in:
*The Guardian*, 17 October 2003

Anmerkungen

1 Oliver Letwin: the Shadow Secretary of State for Economic Affairs and Shadow Chancellor of the Exchequer

2 league tables: dt. Ranglisten

## Lösungsvorschlag

### I. Questions on the text

1. Kirkstone Abbey is a traditional British public school that provides board and lodging. It offers its pupils a classical education (Latin, l. 51) and is organized in Houses, some of which have common dormitories, others single rooms with locks. These Houses are presided over by older students, the 'Heads' and have their own rugby teams. Above the level of 'Heads' are the 'Prefects' who are responsible for discipline and may punish offenders.

2. Parallel to this official hierarchy there is also an unofficial one among the pupils. Some of them derive their importance from bullying the weaker ones.
   James Wheatley is described as a "small" and "wiry" boy with "a clever impish face and shrewd, spiteful eyes" (l. 5) who is constantly looking out for his next victims. He has gathered around him two eager companions who, like him, are prone to bully others. Their actions are sometimes cruel and wide off the mark, as in the case of William Abbot (ll. 9–14). James is intimidating to all except Richard and strikes out arbitrarily.
   Bullying is against the school's rules but seems to be practised widely, in the dorms and in the classrooms. It creates an atmosphere of tension and insecurity and is used to defend the existing order of rank among the pupils.

3. Bullying is strictly not tolerated by the school and would probably be punished severely, especially the serious cases. However, as detection is almost impossible the teachers do not seem to be aware of it. The unwritten rule among the pupils is that nobody complains or tells on the offenders. So when the prefect tries to track down the culprits after the laundry basket episode he finds nobody willing to cooperate. Thus all the authorities can do is impose ineffective collective punishment while bullying cannot be stopped.

4. Jonathan is a quiet and dreamy boy who is always half on the run from James. He seems to feel lonely and friendless (cf. ll. 54 ff.) with no noticeable self-confidence. In his dormitory he feels unhappy and would prefer to be in Abbey House, with a room for himself, because he could lock out unpleasant surprises like being pestered by the bullies, and also because he could have privacy there.
   Jonathan admires Richard, as a kind of role model, for the way he talks to the teachers and for not being scared of James. He is also grateful that Richard has helped him (l. 52 f). Though Richard is apparently not interested in him, he considers trying to become friends with him (l. 54 f.) but, on second thoughts, realizes that Richard, as a strong and independent character, does not need his friendship (l. 62).

5. Patrick Redmond largely uses Jonathan as his third-person-narrator with his limited point of view. Parts of this excerpt use the technique of reported thought (e. g. ll. 56 f.). In two cases Jonathan's thoughts take the form of outcries (ll. 7 and 65), given in italics, in the first example as a fragment without punctuation. So the reader is made to share Jonathan's perceptions, insecurity and fears. Another example of how the limited perspective works is Jonathan's brief reference to what happened to Paul Ellerson (l. 25). By withholding further information from the readers as to the nature of the incident their apprehension is roused as well as their awareness of the general atmosphere of fear.
   This atmosphere is enhanced by the sounds Jonathan tries to pick up and interpret in view of their significance for him. The whisperings and hissings, traces of James' high-pitched voice (ll. 32 ff.) seem to bode evil for him. When James has said good

night he relaxes, the harmless sounds of coughs, sneezes and bedsprings, the water pipe and the wind outside contribute to reduce the tension he and the reader have felt. In the last sentence, however, the author mentions the "heavy silence", which shows that Jonathan is still not quite at ease.

## II. Composition

1. **"I would rather be a coward than brave because people hurt you when you are brave." (E. M. Forster) Discuss.**

   Nobody admires a coward whereas everybody is full of praise for the hero. History records numerous acts of bravery, from the heroic sacrifice of the Spartan king Leonidas and his army to modern-day intrepid astronauts flying the Discovery into space and risking their lives for the benefit of their country or even mankind. The consequences are, more often than not, that they lose their lives but become national heroes and inspiring examples for generations to come. Yet most of us would rather think twice when it comes to face danger, pain or untoward situations with courage and confidence, especially when the odds are heavily against us. If we take sides against our choleric boss we might get fired, if we stand up against a hostile crowd we might get abused or beaten up, if we decide to save a drowning person from the icy water we might drown ourselves. If we retreat or turn away we will not be commended for our valour in the newspaper and will not be awarded a medal but find ourselves part of a huge silent majority and remain unharmed; nobody will know about it and criticize our behaviour. We will return to our home and continue to be role models for our unsuspecting family. But will we also feel good about it? The proverb says that cowards die often – a worldly wisdom, which means that cowards will suffer again and again when they are confronted with a difficult situation.

   There is no general recipe for how to act in a dangerous situation and no guarantee that no harm will follow if we decide to be brave. Maybe a little caution is not altogether the wrong policy but if everybody retreated all the time – how could the world become a better place?

   Not even E. M. Forster is absolutely craven – it takes courage to admit that you are a coward.

2. **"Without friends no one would choose to live though he had all other goods." (Aristotle) What do you think?**

   This quotation from Aristotle sounds rather radical at first glance. What he basically wanted to say is that you will find it difficult to lead a fulfilled and happy life if you haven't got any friends to share it with you. I am positive that he didn't mean friends in the sense of people you know and occasionally keep you company but true, intimate and important friends.

   Real friends are persons you like, who are close to you and who you enjoy spending your time with. Mostly they have known you for long, they have accompanied you through good times and bad ones and have always been there to advise you and to comfort you. They give you a shoulder to cry on when you have problems with your parents or when you are lovesick. They stand by your side when the worst comes to the worst, they fight for you, lie for you and suffer for you – and you would do exactly the same for them. There can be no doubt that friendships are the greatest assets in your life, more than other goods, as Aristotle has it. What is the use of possessions like a luxurious house if you sit there alone, a splendid yacht when you sail it by yourself, a wardrobe full of the latest designer clothes if nobody goes out with you?

   On the other hand there are people Aristotle did not mention and who could, to a certain extent, make up for lack of friends – your family. A father, mother and brothers and sisters are persons who know you even better than friends do and whose loyalty and value for you is beyond doubt. And yet, one day you will become independent of your parents and fend for yourself, you may lose contact with your siblings who will start their own families – and your friends will still be there for you. And this makes them the most important ingredient of a life worth living. I whole-heartedly agree with Aristotle.

3. **Violence at schools has increased over the last few years. Write an article for a quality newspaper in which you analyse the causes and effects of this development.**

*Note: Though you have to pretend to compose an article you can write a traditional essay here. You may introduce your personal opinion to a greater extent as long as you stick to the terms required by a quality newspaper, which means you have to avoid simple and colloquial language. Mind that you consider causes and effects!*
*The following text was written by a student of Max-Planck-Gymnasium, Munich, and is printed here with her permission and slightly adapted. You will see that the 'usual suspects' like media and computer games are not brought up, which is permissible in a newspaper's opinion page.*

Many parents are very particular about supervising every step their offspring has to take to school and back. They are convinced that school is a safe haven and that nothing can happen to their kid once he has entered the school premises.
Alas – in many cases they are wrong! Violence at schools has always been a topic but during the last decade it has become a grave and serious one. The danger is not only some freak who got hold of his dad's gun but a whole army of nagging, teasing, insulting, punching and kicking rascals who are the bane of many children's lives. The second question a parent asks after their kid was beaten up or robbed of his money, right after "Why didn't you tell me earlier?" is "Why do they do this?"
Well, why? Because they are frustrated. Because they are poor. Because their parents have had too little time and money to make them happy, or maybe they just didn't care. Because these children are probably mistreated and beaten at home. Every year misfortune befalls more and more families. More people lose their jobs, become poor, aggressive, addicted to alcohol and even drugs. Yet all the time the world demands more and more of the youths. So they become frustrated and, because they know no better, they take it out on the weaker ones.
The parents of the victims try to send their children to better schools, to private schools, religious schools, boarding schools but the problem remains for the great majority and is even growing. People who experience abuse often become abusers themselves. If we can't break this vicious circle not only our young will get used to violence but it will become part of our whole society with disastrous social and political consequences. I wonder whether George Bush or Lindy England* were bullies at school!
Violence among children and at schools will not decrease if we don't become kinder to each other and more sensitive to other people's misery. It will not stop unless we care!

Anmerkung
* The American soldier who abused Iraqi prisoners

4. **An interview with the Minister of Education. Your topic is: "To what extent does school prepare us for life?**

*Note: The following interview was also written by a student and is printed with her permission and some small alterations.*

ME: Good morning, Mrs. Hohlmeier. I am very grateful to you for granting me this interview after what you must have gone through in recent times. As a previous Minister of Education in Bavaria you can certainly comment on the growing dissatisfaction with the German school system. Critics say that it doesn't prepare students well enough for life at a time when they have to face various challenges when they leave school, such as jobs and social conflicts. Is our school education practical enough?

HOHLMEIER: Yes, definitely! I think it is getting better and better. We require students to look into different careers and businesses where they can practise certain professions to give them an orientation of what they would be like for them. Besides, I am convinced that it is basically education that matters and which supplies the main qualification for getting a job.

ME: But in these days employers ask for much more than just education. They increasingly choose their employees on the basis of their 'soft skills' like social competence, ability to communicate and conflict solving. Does school also give a preparation for these?

HOHLMEIER: But of course! We teach the kids how to behave in a group. We also started a program of mediation to help the kids solve their conflicts on their own. As to social contacts – they develop naturally when so many children are together so much.

ME: But don't you agree that with more extracurricular activities group feeling and social contacts could be intensified?

HOHLMEIER: Yes, maybe. But some responsibilities, such as finding adequate extracurricular activities for their children, must be left to the parents,. There are enough private institutions where they can enrol. I repeat: school equals academic education! What else are you going to ask for – free boarding schools for all?

ME: Well, many people still think school has the obligation to prepare for life and jobs – which are increasingly difficult to get. How do you instruct children to deal with unemployment?

HOHLMEIER: School has the duty to lay the foundation for the future working-life, as you also say. So we can't gear our education to the few who won't find employment, right?

ME: Permit me one last question, Mrs. Hohlmeier. You maintain that the state school system prepares pupils well enough for life but sent your own kids to a private school. Would you comment on that?

HOHLMEIER: I object to that! You are jumping to conclusions! I am afraid my time is up now; I have other matters to attend to.

ME: Well, thank you very much for this interview.

## III. Translation

Oliver Letwins Aussage, dass er eher betteln ginge[1] als seine Kinder auf eine staatliche Gesamtschule am Ort zu schicken, rief eine solche Empörung hervor, dass er sich einige Tage später dafür[1] entschuldigen musste. Doch eigentlich hatte er nur öffentlich ausgesprochen[2], was die meisten Angehörigen seiner Gesellschaftsschicht nicht nur denken, sondern was sie privat auch frei heraus sagen, und was sie natürlich auch in die Tat umsetzen. Es gibt nur[1] sehr wenige Leute, die es sich locker leisten könnten, ihre Kinder auf Privatschulen zu schicken und sich doch[3] dagegen entscheiden.

Es ist leider so, dass viele Leute, die es sich nicht leisten können, ihren Kindern die besondere Erfahrung des Privatschulunterrichts zu ermöglichen, dazu gebracht wurden, den unerschütterlichen Glauben der Mittelschicht[4] zu teilen, dass diese Erfahrung auf geistig höherer Stufe steht. Aber die Ranglisten, auf denen die führenden Privatschulen immer ganz oben stehen, geben ein falsches Bild[5]. Diese Schulen sortieren die schwachen Schüler vor den Prüfungen gnadenlos aus – was diejenigen vergessen[6], die glauben, dass die Public Schools[7] nicht nur besser, sondern auch schülerfreundlicher[8] als die staatlichen Schulen sind.

Die Vorteile jedoch, welche sich die meisten Eltern vom Besuch einer Privatschule erhoffen, sind weniger schulischer als gesellschaftlicher Natur. Die meisten Eltern, die Schulgeld zahlen, kaufen sich in Wirklichkeit nicht eine reichere intellektuelle[9] Erfahrung für ihr Kind, sondern ein ihnen genehmes[10] soziales Umfeld und die Aussicht auf eine künftige entsprechende[7] gesellschaftliche Stellung für ihren Nachwuchs.

Anmerkungen

1 stilistisch bedingte Einfügungen
2 wörtlich: Doch alles was er tatsächlich tat, war öffentlich zu sagen …
3 Das *but* wird hier durch *doch* ausgedrückt.
4 Im Deutschen steht besser der Singular.
5 auch: sind irreführend
6 Die Wiedergabe im Aktiv wirkt hier weniger umständlich.
7 Zusatz zur Verdeutlichung
8 ein geläufiger, hier besser passender Fachausdruck
9 *intellectual* wurde vorher bereits mit *geistig* übersetzt, also kann man hier durchaus beruhigt das Fremdwort verwenden
10 kürzer und treffender für: *they feel comfortable with*

**Leistungskurs Englisch 2006**
**Textaufgabe I**

## Religious right fights science for the heart of America

Al Frisby has spent the better part of his life in rooms filled with rebellious teenagers, but the last years have been particularly trying for the high school biology teacher. He has met parents who want him to teach that God created Eve out of Adam's rib, and who insist that Noah invited dinosaurs aboard the ark. And it is getting more difficult to keep such talk out of the classroom.

"Somewhere along the line, the students have been told the theory of evolution is not valid," he said. "In the last few years, I've had students question my teaching about cell classification and genetics, and there have been comments from students saying: 'Didn't God do that?'" In Kansas, the geographical centre of America, the heart of the American heartland, the state-approved answer might soon be Yes. In the coming weeks, state educators will decide on proposed curriculum changes for high school science put forward by subscribers to the notion of "intelligent design", a modern version of creationism. If the religious right has its way, and it is a powerful force in Kansas, high school science teachers could be teaching creationist material by next September.

Similar classroom confrontations between God and science are under way in 17 states, according to the National Centre for Science Education. In Missouri, state legislators are drafting a bill laying down that science texts contain a chapter on so-called alternative theories to evolution. Textbooks in Arkansas and Alabama contain disclaimers on evolution, and in a Wisconsin school district, teachers are required to instruct their students in the "scientific strengths and weaknesses of evolutionary theory". Last month, a judge in Georgia ordered a school district to remove stickers on school textbooks that warned: "This textbook contains material on evolution. Evolution is a theory, not a fact, regarding the origin of living things."

For the conservative forces engaged in the struggle for America's soul, the true battleground is public education, the laboratory of the next generation, and an opportunity for the religious right to effect lasting change on popular culture. Officially, the teaching of creationism has been outlawed since 1987 when the Supreme Court ruled that the inclusion of religious material in science classes in public teaching was unconstitutional. In recent years, however, opponents of evolution have regrouped, challenging science education with the doctrine of "intelligent design", which has been carefully stripped of all references to God and religion. Unlike traditional creationism, which posits that God created the earth in six days, proponents of intelligent design assert that the workings of this planet are too complex to be ascribed to evolution. There must have been a designer working to a plan – that is, a creator.

In their campaign to persuade parents in Kansas to welcome the new version of creationism into the classroom, subscribers to intelligent design have appealed to a sense of fair play, arguing that it would be in their children's interest to be exposed to all schools of thought on the earth's origins. "We are looking for science standards that would be more informative, that would open the discussion about origins, rather than close it," said John Calvert, founder of the Intelligent Design network.

Other supporters of intelligent design go further, saying evolution is as much an article of faith as creationism. "Certainly there are clear religious implications," said William Harris, a research biochemist and co-founder of the design network in Kansas. "There are creation myths on both sides. Which one do you teach?" During the past five years, subscribers to intelligent design have assembled influential supporters in the state, including a smattering of people with PhDs, such as Mr Harris, to lend their cause a veneer of scientific credibility. When conservative Republicans took control of the Kansas state school board, the creationists seized their chance, installing supporters on the committee reviewing the high school science curriculum.

Jack Krebs, a high school maths teacher on the committee drafting the new standards, argues that the campaign against evolution amounts to a stealth assault on the entire body of scientific thought. "There are two planes where they are attacking. One is evolution, and one is science itself," he said. "They believe that the naturalist bias of science is in fact atheistic. And so this is really an attack on all science."

It would certainly seem so in Kansas. At the first of a series of public hearings on the new course material, the audience was equally split between the defenders of established science and the anti-evolution rebels. In a crowded high school auditorium, biology teachers, mathematicians, a veterinarian, and a high school student made passionate speeches on the need for cold, scientific detachment, and the damage that would be done to the state's reputation and biotechnology industry if Kansas became known as a haven for creationists. They were countered by John James, who warned that the teaching of evolution led to nihilism, and to the gates of Auschwitz. But the largest applause of the evening was reserved for a silver-haired gentleman. "I have a question: if man comes from monkeys, why are there still monkeys? Why do you waste time teaching something in science class that is not scientific?" he thundered.

Science teachers believe that the genteel questioning of the intelligent design movement masks a larger project to discredit an entire body of rational thought. If the Kansas state school board allows science teachers to question evolution, where will it stop? Will religious teachers bring their beliefs into the classroom?

"They are trying to create a climate where anything an individual teacher wants to include in science class can be considered science," said Harry McDonald, a retired biology teacher and president of Kansas Citizens for Science Education. "They want to redefine science."

From an article by Suzanne Goldenberg in: *The Guardian*, 7 February 2005

**Worksheet:**

maximum number of points attainable

## I. Questions on the text

Read all the questions first, then answer them in the given order. Use your own words as far as is appropriate.

1. Examine how Al Frisby's professional experience has changed over the years. — 10
2. Show to what extent creationists and their ideas have been gaining ground within the school systems in Kansas and other American states. — 20
3. Explain in what ways the religious right's notion of creation has been modified over the past twenty years. What, according to the text, prompted this development? — 10
4. Sum up the arguments advocates of intelligent design put forward for this doctrine. Why do they want it to be taught at school? — 20

5. According to the text, what implications for science as such does the current debate in Kansas have? 10
6. Analyse how the text reflects the writer's attitude to creationist ideas. Give evidence from the text. 20
7. Explain the various meanings of the expression "heart" of America as used in the headline and the text (cf. l. 9). 10

## II. Composition

Choose *one* of the following topics. Write about 250 to 300 words. 50

1. There should be no ethical limits to science. Discuss.
2. "The price of freedom of religion, or of speech, or of the press, is that we must put up with a good deal of rubbish." (Robert Jackson) Discuss.
3. Why has religious fundamentalism become so appealing?
4. Interpret the cartoon and answer the question.

From: galleri.magiskamolekyler.org

## III. Translation

Translate the following text into German: 50/200

The new exhibition called "Darwin" at the American Museum of Natural History portrays the making of the man and the scientist, and it reminds us how well and how fully evolution explains the life around us. It also captures the way Darwin's theory opened an entirely new window in the human imagination. It is possible to say, in fact, that humans did not begin to understand their place in nature until 1859.

The exhibition is useful, too, in reminding us that the controversy over evolution has been more or less constant since 1859, though it has reached a peak of political absurdity only in our own time. The basic objections to evolution – the ones trumpeted by the proponents of so-called intelligent design[1] – are essentially the ones Darwin described in the sixth chapter of "Origin"[2]. But Darwin did a surprisingly good job of forestalling his critics. He showed that most of the objections to his theory, then as now, were based on a misunderstanding of the nature of his argument, or were owing simply to the fact that so much remains to be discovered about the workings of life on Earth.

From *The Grandeur of Evolution in a New Exhibition called 'Darwin'*
by Verlyn Klinkenberg in: *The New York Times*, 19 November 2005


Anmerkungen
1 intelligent design: *dt.* Intelligentes Design
2 "Origin": reference to Darwin's book *The Origin of Species,* 1859; *nicht zu übersetzen*

## Lösungsvorschlag

### I. Questions on the text

1. *To answer the question, you should read lines 1–9 carefully.*

   As a biology teacher, Al Frisby has always been used to teaching rebellious students, but in the last years it has become more and more difficult to resist the wishes of parents who want him to include biblical teachings in the classroom. And students who have been told that the theory of evolution is wrong, increasingly call his teachings into question by attributing everything to God's creation.

2. *The relevant information is to be found from line 9 ("In Kansas ...") to 22 ("... origin of living things."). Note that the article was written in February 2005 – in the meantime the State Board of Education in Kansas has approved of the mentioned changes. The question, however, refers to the article.*

   In Kansas state educators are planning to introduce "intelligent design" – a modern version of creationism – into the science curriculum. According to the National Center for Science Education, similar attempts are being made in 17 other states, among them Missouri, where legislation is prepared that alternative theories to evolution have to be included in science textbooks. In Wisconsin teachers have to teach about the strengths and weaknesses of evolution, and in Arkansas and Alabama textbooks reject evolution altogether. Finally, a school in Georgia put stickers on textbooks telling students that "Evolution is a theory, not a fact ..." (l. 22). They had to be removed, however, after a court ruling.

3. *In the second paragraph the writer says that "intelligent design" is a modern version of creationism (l. 12). In the fourth paragraph he explains that this development was prompted by a decision of the Supreme Court in 1987 (ll. 27/28).*

   Traditional creationism used to interpret the Bible literally and argued that God created the world in six days. After the Supreme Court had outlawed its teaching in public schools by ruling in 1987 that religious instruction in science classes was unconstitutional, the opponents of evolution began to gather around the proponents of "intelligent design", a modern version of creationism that has been rid of all references to God and religion. This new theory concludes that certain features of the universe are too complex to be explained by evolution, so it is highly probable that there is an intelligent designer behind it.

4. *Read the question and text carefully. The arguments put forward in the text are rather why 'intelligent design' should be treated on equal terms with evolution than arguments to back up the doctrine. The second sentence makes it clear that you are to summarize the <u>arguments</u> of the advocates <u>for teaching</u> their doctrine at school. They are mostly mentioned in the 5th to 8th paragraphs (lines 35–65). The reasons for the battle about what is to be taught in school, however, is already mentioned at the beginning of the 4th paragraph (l. 24ff).*

   Some proponents of 'intelligent design' pretend that their theory is equal to evolution and that it would only be fair to open up a discussion about all theories on the earth's origins.

   Others go even further and distance themselves from evolution, which they see – just like creationism – as an article of faith or a kind of religion. To them there are clear "myths" in evolution, which they regard just as an unproven theory.

   Finally, there are those who suspect science to be atheistic and think that the teaching of evolution would lead to nihilism and finally to Auschwitz.

If they want to achieve a lasting change in America's culture, the adherents of the religious right know that they must win the minds of the next generation. That's why they concentrate a lot of their efforts on public schools.

5. *Before you answer the question read the 7th (l. 50ff) and the last two paragraphs (l. 66ff) carefully. You should have no difficulty giving an answer like this:*

   According to science teachers, the supporters of 'intelligent design' intend to discredit science altogether by calling evolution into question. They are trying to redefine it so that individual convictions can be taught as science in school. All in all, they regard natural science as atheistic and are trying to replace it by religion.

6. *This is certainly meant to be an* ***expository*** *text, i. e. a text that wants to* ***inform*** *the reader about the current debate on evolution and intelligent design in parts of the USA. Ideally, such an article should be objective and leave it to the readers to draw their conclusions. If you look closely at this text, however, you will easily find that the author's* ***choice of words, images****, the* ***rhetorical devices*** *he employs and his* ***use of quotations*** *reveal which side he is on.*

   The author is very critical of "intelligent design" if not altogether against it. For him it is only "a modern version of creationism" (l. 12) His attitude becomes already clear by his choice of words in the very first paragraph. Instead of simply stating that parents want Frisby to teach creationism he tries to show how foolish these people are by interpreting the Bible literally. So they want him to teach in the science classroom that "God created Eve out of Adam's rib" (l. 3) or that "Noah invited dinosaurs aboard the ark." (l. 4). In the same way, he does not speak of a confrontation between evolution and 'intelligent design', but "between God and science." (l. 15)
   Then he quotes only the most stupid supporters of the "intelligent design" theory. "Didn't God do that?" (ll. 8/9) is certainly not scientific reasoning, and the question "… if man comes from monkeys, why are there still monkeys?" (ll. 63/64) is at best naive. On the other hand, the representatives of evolution he quotes, like Jack Krebs (ll. 50 ff.) or Harry McDonald (ll. 71 ff.), are serious scientists who argue rationally.
   His imagery portrays the proponents of "intelligent design" as a belligerent lot. They are "conservative forces" (l. 24), whose "battleground" (ll. 24/25) is the school; they "have regrouped" (l. 29) after a defeat and are preparing a "stealth assault" (l. 51) on scientific thought.
   Finally, at the end of the text, the author uses rhetorical questions to illustrate the danger he sees in the movement: "… if … Kansas … allows teachers to question evolution, where will it stop?" (ll. 67/68)

7. *Consult your dictionary before you set out to answer. The following entries for 'heart' will be helpful:*
   *– the part of you that feels strong emotions and feelings*
   *– the most important or central part of something*
   *– the centre of an area*
   *– the thoughts, emotions and attitudes of people*
   *Your answer may now read like this:*

   When you read the headline, you think that it is a fight for the emotions and attitudes, or as some people will say, for the souls of Americans. In lines 9–10, however, the writer refers to Kansas as "America's heartland". He says that it is the "geographical center" of America (l. 9). The wording "the heart of America's heartland" (ll. 9/10), however, suggests that this is the part where America is most American, probably most conservative and most likely to adopt the ideas of the religious right. It is the crucial part, because if the battle against evolution is lost at its 'heart', it will be lost everywhere else in America.

## II. Composition

1. *Consulting your dictionary may again help you. The entry 'ethical issues/questions/ problems' gives you the following example: "The use of animals in scientific tests raises difficult ethical questions." (DCE) The same is, of course, true for genetic engineering or cloning.*

   Some scientists argue that there should be no limits to scientific work. They think that mankind can benefit most from it if there is no interference. They see genetic engineering as a case in point. Although viewed sceptically by the general public, they point out that with its help they will soon be able to understand diseases better and develop new effective treatments. Genetically engineered crops can help us to cope with the problem of overpopulation and feeding the masses in the Third World. All this, the proponents argue, could not be achieved if the opponents had their way and restricted scientific research.

   But very often scientists are blind to the larger consequences of their work. In their enthusiam they do not see the dangers involved in their pursuits. What if – as a result of genetic manipulation – the new crops will pose a threat to the ecosystem of the planet? Ecologists warn that whole groups of plants and insects might become extinct as a result of genetic engineering. Or take the effects the science might have on our society: will people start to select only babies who conform to the norms of our society? Will there be cloning of humans – can there be a whole new generation of Hitlers? A lot of opponents think that the individual states should impose ethical limits and prevent scientists from carrying out such dangerous experiments. But that is not really a solution – just think how a lot of regimes like the Nazis violated medical ethics.

   Of course, we will never be able to eliminate the abuse of scientific research completely, but scientists and renowned people from all walks of life should try and form ethics committees to create guidelines for research on a national as well as on the international level.

2. *Any supporter of these freedoms would of course agree with Robert Jackson, who was the chief United States prosecutor at the Nuremberg Trials (1946) and knew what the repression of freedom would lead to.*
   *To take a critical look at the quotation, however, you may ask yourself if we also have to put up with racist progaganda, blasphemy, hate speech or pornography.*

   When the Danish newspaper Jyllands-Posten published a number of Muhammad cartoons in 2005, Muslims all over the world were up in arms against what they considered blasphemous drawings, intended to humiliate them and their religion. The editors and cartoonists, however, argued that they only exercised their rights of free speech and of freedom of the press in an age of Islamic extremist terrorism. They had also run satirical cartoons depicting Christian figures, they said. So do we really have to put up with everything in papers and magazines, or are there any limits to what can be published?

   A lot of people in Western countries would like to introduce new laws against hate speech, Nazi propaganda and support of terrorists. Others would like to ban so-called religious groups like Scientology or cults like Heaven's Gate. They see all their activities as dangerous to the cohesion of our society.

Of course, the right of freedom of the press, or of speech, does not mean that we can insult, discriminate against and degrade others. Nor does freedom of religion mean that those groups can abuse their adherents physically or mentally or even violate the laws of the society. But as long as there are no such violations we certainly have to put up with all sorts of publications, opinions and so-called religions.
The Danish Muhammad cartoons may serve as a case in point: what one side sees as humiliation, the other side regards as a legitimate expression of opinion in a current controversy. In a democratic state freedom is such an important value that we should not make any compromises. As some observers of the conflict said: "The cartoons are at best mediocre, but we have to defend the right of the cartoonists to be mediocre." In other words, we have to put up with a lot, even if it is rubbish.

3. *It may help you to consult your dictionary. Fundamentalism is defined as "the practice of following very strictly the basic rules and teachings of any religion" or (in Christianity) as "the belief that everything that is written in the Bible is completely true". (Advanced Learner's Dictionary)*
*Starting from this definition, you can now say why you think this is particularly appealing to a lot of people. There is no easy answer to the question – we can only try to give one (e. g. simplicity of explanations in an increasingly complicated world, charismatic leaders, security for the adherent, etc.).*

It is certainly true to say that fundamentalist movements, i. e. movements that interpret their sacred texts such as the the Qu'ran or the Bible literally and strictly follow their teachings, are on the upswing today. Radical Islamic groups exist throughout the Middle East and in many countries in Africa and Asia, and we can find Christian fundamentalists in various Western countries, but especially in the United States.
What makes them so attractive to a lot of people today? In the case of Islamic extremism the answer seems to be easy. After their defeat in the wars with Israel in the 1960s and 70s, a lot of Muslims realized that their status in the world was diminished and felt humiliation and anger at the situation. Charismatic leaders like Osama bin Laden blame the corrupt West for their predicament and keep promising the adherents that they can overcome their plight by concentrating on their – superior – religion.
But that is only part of the story. Even though both groups object to being put into the same category, there seem to be some similarities between the attraction of Christian and Islamic fundamentalist groups. Our modern world has become so complicated and difficult to understand, and science and technology have created as many problems as they have solved. So a lot of people lack orientation in today's world and long for some everlasting truth. And they long for some kind of corporate feeling, which they can find in a community with like-minded people. Fundamentalist religions claim to know eternal truths from the scripture, and very often charismatic leaders make the world understandable and thus give their devotees a feeling of security.

4. *The cartoon is reminiscent of the evolution charts used in biology classrooms. The second part of the title of this essay refers to the meaning or purpose of life and can, of course, be answered in very different ways.*

The present cartoon looks at first sight like one of the charts that we all know from our biology classrooms. It shows the development of life on earth from the time when amphibians first got from the sea onto the land, then there are reptiles as the next stage of evolution, after them we see a kind of monkey as the first mammal, and finally there is man. All creatures that inhabited the planet before human beings took their lives for granted and were content to eat and to multiply. Only man, who is the last and most sophisticated link of this chain, wonders what "it is all about". It is ironical, then, that human beings, who are supposed to be of higher intelligence than all their predeces-

sors, should the first to be confused by such a question. Not content with "eating, surving and reproducing" man is at a loss to answer the question about the meaning or purpose of life.
There is, of course, no simple answer. A large number of indifferent people would just say that their purpose in life is to seek happiness through accumulating wealth and increasing their social status. But lots of philosophers since Socrates' time have tried to establish systems of values for man to live by. Atheists will say that, since there is no god, it depends on how we determine the nature of life. Religious people, far from being content with the Old Testament's "Be fruitful and multiply", would say that only God can give their lives a meaning and a purpose. Where all of us should agree in my opinion is that "it is all about" loving our fellow-beings, living in peace with one another and in harmony with the environment and that we should strive to create good and just societies to live in.

## III. Translation

Die neue Ausstellung im American Museum of Natural History, die den Titel „Darwin" trägt, zeigt den Werdegang dieses Mannes und Wissenschaftlers und sie erinnert uns daran, wie gut und wie vollständig die Evolutionstheorie[1] das Leben um uns herum erklärt. Sie hält auch fest, wie Darwins Theorie ein völlig neues Fenster der menschlichen Vorstellungskraft eröffnete. Man kann wirklich sagen, dass die Menschen erst 1859 anfingen, ihren Platz in der Natur zu verstehen.
Diese Ausstellung ist auch nützlich, indem sie uns daran erinnert, dass die Kontroverse[2] über die Evolution seit 1859 mehr oder weniger unvermindert andauert, obwohl sie erst in unserer Zeit einen Gipfel politischer Unsinnigkeit[3] erreicht hat. Die grundlegenden Einwände gegen die Evolutionstheorie – die von den Befürwortern des so genannten „Intelligenten Designs" lautstark verkündet werden – sind im Grunde genommen dieselben, die Darwin im sechsten Kaptitel seines Werks[4] „Origin" beschrieben hat. Aber Darwin ist seinen Kritikern auf überraschend gute Weise zuvorgekommen. Er zeigte, dass die meisten Einwände gegen seine Theorie – damals wie heute – auf einem Missverständnis über das Wesen seiner Argumentation[5] beruhen oder einfach auf die Tatsache zurückzuführen sind, dass erst noch[6] vieles über die Wirkungsweise des Lebens auf der Erde entdeckt werden muss.

Anmerkungen

1 Im Deutschen sollte man den Begriff zu ‚*Evolutionstheorie*' erweitern.
2 Da ‚*Kontroverse*' ein Fachausdruck ist, kann man das Fremdwort hier stehen lassen. Deutsche Alternative: ‚*Streit*'
3 ‚*Absurdität*' wird natürlich auch anerkannt
4 Zusatz zur Verdeutlichung
5 „*argument*" bezieht sich auf Darwins Argumentation; der Singular ‚*Argument*' wäre hier falsch
6 Zusatz zur Verdeutlichung

## Leistungskurs Englisch 2006
## Textaufgabe II

*A scene between William Kemp and his nephew, Matthew Paris:*

They were in the room on the first floor of the house which Kemp regarded as his sanctum and sometimes called his study, though nothing much but ledgers were studied there. Pipe in mouth, he looked through curls of smoke at the young man sitting opposite, hunched forward in the easy-chair as if set on maintaining a notion of sufferance, his large hands loosely clasped between his knees. "You must regard my house as your own for as long as you choose," he said.

The sound of his own words animated Kemp with a renewed sense of the excellence of his motives. His spirits rose. He was behaving generously towards his nephew and at the same time gaining the services of a qualified medical man. A less qualified medical man would have done, he knew that: most of the slavers that sailed out of Liverpool would have some sawbones' apprentice or drunken quack aboard, or no one; but that was not good enough for the *Liverpool Merchant.* Moreover, he was killing other pigeons with the same shot: by this kindness to a bankrupt he was dressing his ship in the colours of charity and compassion.

Kemp held a moral view of the universe. God balanced the ledgers. Nothing went unrecognised. A good deed was an entry on the credit side, a bill drawn on destiny which could not fail to be met one day. He saw his ship home in port again, riding at anchor in the Pool, laden with goods high in demand, saw his creditors satisfied, temporarily at least, with the interest on their loans, till the cotton trade took a turn for the better, as it soon must. The vision glowed in his cheeks and eyes as he leaned forward. "Africa," he said, "you will be going to Africa, Matthew. Think of it."

"I have thought much of it." Paris sat up a little, straightening his shoulders in polite response. He did not know what to say to his uncle, whom he thought looked rather hectic and high-coloured this afternoon, feverish almost; he would have liked to take his pulse.

Not feeling able to suggest this, he looked away towards the window.

*By the river, Ruth and I hand in hand, light raining down on leaf and bud, shadows moving on the water. Light of love in her face. We sat together on the bank. By then she was carrying the child. A day to be remembered, because we knew – and told each other – that we need do nothing but wait. We only had to be as we were. Everything was calm and satisfactory. The house not very grand but with room enough, and the income from shop and practice sufficient. We only had to wait, with our love, for the child to come. Now Ruth is nowhere in the world any more and I am going to Africa.*

"Yes," he said, "well, it is very far away. It is a place I had never thought to visit. But it might as well be there as anywhere." Lest this should sound ungrateful, he added quickly, "I thank you once again for your letter, uncle, and for wishing to do me a service."

"Blood is thicker than water." Kemp's tone held an increased alertness. He had sensed some reservation in the other's words. "You did yourself express an interest in what I had to propose," he added after a short pause. After all, it is why you are here, he was on the point of adding, but refrained, as it might seem to suggest there could be no other reason. All the same, the question hung in the air for some moments. Paris did not reply immediately. He was a man who, Kemp suspected, might gnaw at his own purposes indefinitely if left alone to do so.

"You have taken into account the advantages, of course," he said. "As I outlined them in my letter. You will be calling at places with many marvels to offer."

"Indeed yes." Paris nodded gravely. "It was said by Pliny[1] that out of Africa there comes always something new."

"Oh, aye, was it? Well, he was in the right of it. And then, being a man of science you will find a quantity of things to notice."

"I have no doubt of it."

"I don't mention money," the merchant said. "You have incurred expenses and these have been met. We need say no more about that. But there is something else which I think will interest you." Kemp leaned forward again, marking a pause. "I had been keeping it till the ship's articles were signed, but there is no harm in telling you now. I am purposing to allow you three Negroes privilege[2] to be paid out of the cargo at cost, your choice of the blacks to be marked at the time of purchase. There now, what do you think of that?" He was disappointed to discern no change of expression on his nephew's face. "That is in addition to salary," he added in a tone of reproach.

After a long moment Paris smiled slightly and said, "That is an unlooked-for generosity on your part."

"And then, just now, a break, a period away from home, new fields of endeavour. To dispel those unfortunate associations which must … to an extent at least …. I had hoped to have your final answer."

"Oh, I am going," the other replied quickly and, it seemed, almost carelessly, certainly not as though capitulating to argument. In fact he had known from the first, from first receiving his uncle's letter, that he would go. This exile of a long voyage, a commerce he had every reason to believe degraded, and suitable therefore for such as himself – it was a combination, in his wretchedness, impossible to resist. He had not doubted since then, was so far from doubting now that he was surprised to see relief show on his uncle's face. "Certainly, I am going," he repeated.

From: Barry Unsworth, *Sacred Hunger*. London: Penguin 1992

1 Pliny: Pliny the Elder (23 to 79 AD): Roman scholar and scientist

2 privilege: *here:* a customary payment or gratuity to the master of a ship, usually in return for or in anticipation of some service

**Worksheet:**

maximum number of points attainable

## I. Questions on the text

Read all the questions first, then answer them in the given order. Use your own words as far as is appropriate.

1. Outline Kemp's business venture and the current state of his affairs. 10
2. Summarise the arguments used by Kemp to persuade his nephew to accept his offer of the post of the ship's doctor. 20
3. Analyse Kemp's real motives for his offer to Matthew; what do they reveal about his character? 20
4. Outline Matthew's situation in life, past and present, and explain why it accounts for his decision to accept his uncle's offer. 20

5. Choose two examples that reveal how little real communication takes place between the two men in this scene and explain them in detail. 10
6. How do narrative techniques contribute to the reader's perception of the characters? 20

## II. Composition

Choose *one* of the following topics. Write about 250 to 300 words. 50

1. Modern forms of slavery.
2. Slavery and colonialism are not ancient or foreign history; the world they made is around us. Discuss, using your knowledge of British and/or American history.
3. Are moral integrity and economic profit compatible?
4. Write Matthew's letter to a Member of Parliament, protesting against the conditions on board the slave ship, which were similar to the ones in the picture.

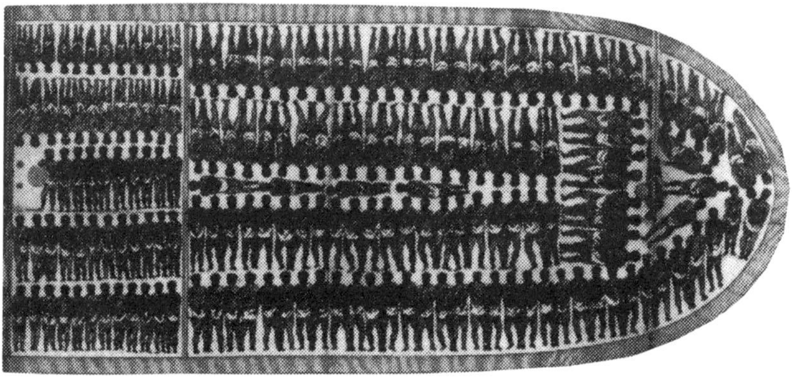

The interior of a slave ship
From: www.blues.is/saga.htm

## III. Translation

Translate the following text into German: 50/200

It is almost obligatory these days to be cynical about those who want to be good. We seem incapable of attributing noble motives to anyone: politicians must be looking to posterity, the rich and successful must be alleviating their guilt or feeding their egos. […]

I have no problem with doing good things for less than pure reasons. So what if a charity record helps promote a singer or band, or if donating money helps ease someone's conscience? Who cares if a political leader is looking to the history books when trying to improve the plight of the world's poor? Every day the rest of us make decisions based on ego and self-interest. Christmas may be the season for giving but the underlying promise of Christianity is that by doing good Christians ensure themselves a place in heaven – a more naked plea to self-interest would be hard to imagine. Rather than falling for the fantasy that selfishness is somehow sinful, we could all do with being more selfish. After all, charity is most effective when it makes a connection with our own lives and our own concerns. The most compelling reason for helping others is that we are also helping ourselves.

From *Be selfish: do a good deed* by Sarfraz Manzoor in:
*The Guardian*, 15 December 2004

## Lösungsvorschlag

### I. Questions on the text

1. *The information you need is to be found in the second and third paragraphs.*

   Mr Kemp is the owner of the slave ship 'Liverpool Merchant'. It sails on the triangular trade route from Liverpool to Africa where slaves are bought, then to America to sell them, and back to England with cotton and other goods. Though this is an extremely lucrative business, the prices for cotton seem to have dropped (l. 19). Mr Kemp still owes money to investors and hopes to appease them with the gains of the next voyage.

2. *Here you only need to summarise, not to analyse his tactics.*

   Mr Kemp insinuates that he wants to do a favour to a member of his family (l. 37) who has suffered a personal loss and needs new perspectives (ll. 61 f.). He emphasises that Matthew himself has shown an interest in his suggestion (ll. 38 f.). The trip, he points out, will give him a chance to see the marvels of the black continent to satisfy his scientific curiosity (l. 45, 48 f.). Kemp also appeals to his nephew's sense of gratitude – he has paid his debts – (l. 51) and mentions the financial aspect: he will pay him a salary and offers him three slaves he can sell at a profit (ll. 54 ff.). As a last argument, he suggests that Matthew could more easily forget his misfortunes with a new challenge (ll. 61 f.).

3. *You will find references to Kemp's motives in paragraphs two and three. Make sure to interpret them, and do not forget to draw conclusions about his character.*

   His motives seem to be based on both benevolence and practical considerations. On the one hand, he offers his bankrupt relative the possibility to make some money and take his mind off his despair. On the other hand, he will be able to hire a competent surgeon and possibly raise the survival rate of his 'goods'. Though he is pleased about "the excellence of his motives", (ll. 7 f.) his generosity to Paris is not a mere act of altruism. He expects to be rewarded by his creator (ll. 16 f.) and that his ignoble slave-trading will be morally upgraded by his "charity and compassion" (l. 14).
   Mr Kemp appears insincere, calculating, and hypocritical. His "moral view of the universe" is a venal system of bookkeeping where God "balanced the ledgers" (l. 15).

4. *This double question requires you to look for information about Matthew's previous history and present situation <u>and</u> to show how this affects his decision.*

   Matthew is a "qualified medical man" (l. 9) who had his own practice and a shop, enough to provide him with a reasonable income and peace of mind (ll. 30 ff.). He had been very much in love with his wife Ruth, who was expecting their baby. She must have lost it and died at childbirth (l. 33). This apparently made him so desperate that he neglected his career and went bankrupt (l. 13). Now he finds himself in an emotionally and financially precarious situation.
   In his uncle's proposal he might see the chance to start a new life but this consideration plays no part in his decision. He seems to blame himself for his misfortune and welcomes his participation in Kemp's wicked business venture as an "exile", a suitable punishment, and an adequate setting for a worthless person like himself (ll. 66 ff.).

5. *There are several examples you can choose from (ll. 23 ff., 39 ff., 59 f., 69 f.) which show how the two men have difficulty in saying what they really want to, misunderstand each other, or cannot keep up a natural conversation.*

The whole conversation is lacking in warmth and familiarity, and is marked by hesitation and pauses. This can be seen in the following examples.

- When Kemp rather abruptly asks his nephew to think of Africa (ll. 21 f.) he gets the wooden response "I have much thought of it" (l. 22), and then Matthew is at a loss to say anything else. He notices that his uncle looks unwell and "would have liked to take his pulse" (ll. 23 f.) but feels too inhibited to propose this and averts his glance to the window.
- Matthew thanks his uncle for his offer "quickly" to avoid the impression of ungratefulness (ll. 35 f.). Kemp feels that something was left unsaid. He tries to make clear that Matthew had after all been interested in the proposal but he does not dare to do emphasise the point. There is "a short pause", and "the question [hung] in the air" (l. 41).

6. *You can find more information about narrative techniques in* ***Tips for Questions on the Text*** *(p. VIII) and in* ***Stichwortverzeichnis III*** *(point of view).*

In the second and third paragraphs, the author narrates exclusively from the perspective of William Kemp, in reported thought. The reader gets the impression that Kemp is a scheming and hypocritical slave-trader who is more interested in his business than in his nephew. This technique is continued in lines 37 to 43, when Kemp's unspoken thoughts reveal his mastery in judging people's reactions and manipulating them.
The passage in italics (ll. 27–33) stands out as a flashback in time where Matthew's memories are presented directly and intensely, in interior monologue. Here the reader gets a first-hand report of Matthew's fall from happiness and comprehends his despair.
In the last paragraph, Matthew's thoughts are reported, in the third person. The author's intention is to make the reader understand that the young man feels guilty and has convinced himself that being a party to the morally degrading enterprise is what he deserves.

## II. Composition

1. *It is always useful to consult the dictionary for definitions of key words, in this case 'slave' and 'slavery'. You will find two useful meanings for 'slave': the obvious one and one that explains a slave as 'a person who is so strongly influenced by something that they cannot live without it, or cannot make their own decisions' (OALD, 7th ed.). Although traditional forms of slavery probably still exist, we recommend to write about the other kind – the dependence of people on e. g. fashion, drugs, work, gambling or computer games.*

Everyone is familiar with the sad history of slavery, when people were owned by 'masters' and forced to do unpaid service. While this form of slavery is no longer associated with the modern world, there are still a variety of situations in which people become enslaved and cannot make their own decisions.
What comes to mind is, for example, the doting lover whose only purpose in life is to dedicate all his efforts to please the object of his obsession. Having completely lost his own will to make decisions, he becomes a true slave of passion. Another well-known figure, even in our classrooms, is the slave of fashion. Who has not met people who would be deeply ashamed to be caught in last season's clothes? They would never wear anything that is just comfortable, practical, or good-looking but slavishly submit themselves to the dictatorship of the fashion industry. Another, more miserable example, is the drug addict, who is incapable of renouncing the use of tobacco, liquor, or

narcotics, even with the consequence of ruining their health and their lives. Nowadays, when work is no longer considered only as a means of earning one's bread and affording a decent life, the workaholic makes it the sole justification of his existence. They are blind to the toll their habit takes on their well-being. The gambler today no longer needs millions to play with; even people with modest incomes succumb to the kick of risking their future in the casino or with online bets. Among the younger generation many have become addicted to computer games, play for hours on end, are immersed in fantasy worlds, and care nothing for school or relationships.
While the old slavery exploited innocent victims of external forces, the more modern forms originate from people's inner weaknesses. Uncle Tom had to die to shatter his bonds – in the case of our modern slaves, there is the chance that reason or the services of a good psychiatrist will help to break their habits.

2. *The most obvious consequence of colonialism, as far as Britain is concerned, is the existence of English-speaking nations around the globe and their continuing economic dependence. Although the US also controlled and colonised foreign areas in a small scale they could not really be considered as a colonial power. In their case, the most striking repercussion is the presence of a strong black minority through the absorption of African slaves into their ethnic structure. You can work on both aspects or limit yourself to one country.*
*Historical note: Colonialism is defined as the occupation of foreign areas or countries to settle there. It took place in several phases after the discovery of America in 1492 starting with Spain and Portugal and followed by the Dutch, the English and the French. Its last epoch was the Age of Imperialism, from around 1870 to the 1940s, when other countries like Germany, Italy and Belgium also established themselves overseas. After World War II, practically all colonies reached their political independence.*
*Slavery dates back to ancient history and reached its climax when the Spanish, Portuguese and Americans imported ca. 30 million African slaves between 1500 and 1860. The slave trade was officially abolished in England in 1807, slavery in 1833, and in the US after the Civil War, in 1866. Though it is outlawed in the statutes of the United Nations, it is supposed to linger on in remote areas.*

At its height, the British Empire included a quarter of the world's population and 'the sun never set upon it'. British merchants were heavily involved in the slave trade until 1807 when it was abolished. It has left no visible traces in their former colonies. Britain had to give up her colonies and has since been presiding over the Commonwealth. The legacy of her history of colonisation has shaped the modern world. In most of her former colonies, English has remained the official language and has established itself as the world's undisputed lingua franca. British culture has left its marks in African, Asian and Caribbean countries, where children still wear school uniforms and families take their tea breaks. Many authors like N. S. Naipaul, Salman Rushdie, or Hanif Kureishi write in English and were awarded prestigious literary prizes. There has also been a notable influence in the field of traditional English sports. Rugby is the most popular sport in New Zealand, Indian and Pakistani cricket teams regularly beat the English, and soccer is played everywhere – so successfully that even Trinidad and Tobago qualified for the World Cup 2006. Politically, the English form of government is still the model for their former colonies, even when some countries have difficulties in implementing democratic standards. Misrule and dictatorial governments are still found in states where corrupt leaders enrich themselves and misuse their power, despite the criticism of most Commonwealth members. Many politicians in the Third World still blame their former colonial powers for their economic plight. They claim

that these countries still exploit their resources and impede their economic progress with trade barriers and unfair prices.
The history of colonialism has shaped our modern world and cannot be undone. Britain, through immigration from former colonies, has become a multicultural society, a fact that is increasingly accepted and even welcomed. In the USA, descendants of former slaves constitute a strong minority in their ethnic mix. The time when an Afro-American will be elected president is not too far away.

3. *You could open your composition by giving an example from your own experience or from press reports. Another possibility would be to present and explain Proudhon's famous statement that "property is theft". In the end, you will have to answer the topical question on the basis of your main part.*

   Josef Ackermann, CEO of Deutsche Bank, became the bogeyman in Germany when, as chairman of the board, he awarded exorbitant compensations to Mannesmann managers who had just liquidated their company. The public outcry became even louder when he announced huge profits and, at the same time, the layoff of thousands of employees. Many people ask themselves whether rising profits lead to sinking morals.
   Since the beginning of the industrial era critics, especially from the socialist side of the political spectrum, have been convinced that commercial and industrial leaders unscrupulously exploit their workers to maximise their gains, by making them work long hours, paying ridiculous wages, and firing them at will. They are suspected of cheating even each other, and selling low-quality products at outrageous prices. Cases where moral considerations are ignored when profits can be increased are often brought to our notice. Who has not heard of builders who bribe to get a contract, or of companies that tolerate child labour in poor countries to cut costs, or pharmaceutical corporations that decided not to produce much needed drugs because profits would be too low?
   On the other hand, the majority of businesses have subscribed to the code of corporate governance, which requires companies to observe the overall good of all constituents – management, employees and the community at large. This includes social responsibility, fair treatment of workers, and respect for the environment. Many firms contribute to charities and sponsor social and cultural programmes. Individual tycoons like Bill Gates, or wealthy celebrities like Jürgen Klinsmann are known to support welfare organisations on a large scale.
   As long as unethical conduct is not rigorously banned by legal restrictions, the temptation to stop at nothing to make a profit cannot be completely prevented. It is a sign of hope that even the corporate world are turning up their noses at Mr Ackermann's behaviour.

4. *This is a formal letter, in which you should give the addresses of yourself and the addressee. Contractions should be avoided as well as colloquialisms. If you can you may try to express yourself in an old-fashioned way.*
   *Start by making a list of the inhuman conditions you as the ship's doctor want to expose, such as accommodation, ill treatment, food, diseases and injuries, survival rate, and expand these keywords in a mind map for details. End by complaining and asking the MP to do what he can to alter conditions on slave ships or even help to abolish slavery.*
   *Historically, in 1789, a committee of the House of Commons investigated the issue but only in 1807 the slave trade slavery was officially abolished in Britain.*

The Right Honourable
William Merriweather MP
The House of Commons

22 Mersey Gardens
Liverpool
12 May 1788

Dear Sir

It has come to my attention that a Parliamentary Committee is being instituted to investigate conditions on slave ships. As the surgeon on board the 'Liverpool Merchant', recently returned from Africa, I would like to protest against what I had the misfortune to observe and offer myself as an eyewitness.

The ship I served on is licensed to carry a maximum number of 450 but started its return voyage with 602 slaves alone, of which 207 died at sea, despite my untiring efforts to preserve their lives. The poor creatures were packed together on the lower deck, secured by leg irons, and hardly able to move. When they were thrown about in heavy sea injuries were common. Women and children were kept in separate quarters and exposed to brutal violence and sexual abuse by the crew. The air in the holds was unfit for respiration due to insufficient ventilation, lack of sanitation, heat and the effects of seasickness. I constantly had to fight fevers and dysentery. When 30 captives were found with the symptoms of smallpox they were thrown overboard alive, against my protests. The food rations dished out twice daily were meagre and often spoiled. Prisoners who refused to eat were severely flogged and force-fed all the same. In good weather, they were brought on deck to perform a mockery of an exercise, whether they were capable of doing so or not.

I can only give a short account of what happened but, as aforesaid, I would like to testify in person and in much more detail. The brutal cruelty and degrading conditions on British slave ships are a disgrace to a Christian nation like ours. I pray that Parliament will outlaw these practices once and for all. It would, however, be even more dignified if slavery as such could be abolished altogether.

Yours faithfully
Matthew Paris, M.D.

## III. Translation

Heutzutage ist man schon fast verpflichtet, sich über diejenigen zynisch zu äußern, die gute Menschen sein wollen. Wir sind anscheinend nicht in der Lage[1] irgendjemandem edle Beweggründe zu unterstellen – es muss einfach[2] so sein, dass Politiker auf die Nachwelt schielen[3], dass die Begüterten und Erfolgreichen ihre Schuldgefühle kompensieren[4] oder ihre Egos pflegen.

Ich habe kein Problem damit, Gutes nicht nur aus lauteren Motiven zu tun. Was ist schon dabei, wenn eine Wohltätigkeitsplatte einem Sänger oder einer Band zu mehr Werbung, oder jemandem Geldspenden zur Erleichterung seines Gewissens verhelfen?[5] Wen kümmert es, wenn ein führender Politiker[6] mit Blick[7] auf die Geschichtsbücher versucht, das Elend der Armen dieser[2] Welt zu lindern? Wir Anderen treffen täglich Entscheidungen auf der Grundlage unseres Egos und unserer Eigeninteressen[8]. Weihnachten mag die Zeit der Geschenke[9] sein, aber es ist das unterschwellige Versprechen des Christentums, dass Christen sich durch gute Werke einen Platz im Himmel sichern können[2] – man kann sich nur[2] schwer einen unverhohleneren Appell an den Eigennutz vorstellen. Anstatt der Vorstellung zu unterliegen, dass Selbstsucht irgendwie eine Sünde ist, könnten wir es alle vertragen, eigennütziger zu sein. Immerhin ist die Wohltätigkeit am wirksamsten, wenn sie sich mit unserem eigenen Leben[10] und unseren eigenen Anliegen verbindet. Das durchschlagendste Motiv dafür anderen zu helfen ist, dass wir damit[2] auch uns selbst helfen.

Anmerkungen

1 Es ist oft eleganter, ein Adjektiv substantivisch zu übersetzen.
2 Stilistisch bedingte Einfügungen oder Änderungen
3 ‚Schielen' scheint uns etwas treffender als ‚schauen'.
4 ‚alleviate', wörtlich ‚erleichtern'; ‚kompensieren' ist wohl eher der Fachausdruck.
5 ‚promote', wörtlich fördern, bekannt machen
6 Umkehrung und Wechsel der Wortarten
7 Hier wurde ein Verb *(looking)* substantiviert wiedergegeben.
8 Im Deutschen ist der Plural angemessener.
9 Dieselbe Übersetzungstechnik wie in Anm. 7.
10 ‚lives' – im Deutschen ist nur der Singular möglich, daher muss er auch bei ‚concerns' stehen.

## Leistungskurs Englisch 2007
## Textaufgabe I

### Taking liberties

What the war on terror and the war on anti-social behaviour have in common

What's a government to do when faced with a bunch of undesirables whose guilt is difficult to prove in a court of justice? Lock them up without a proper trial, of course.

That's how the British government is dealing with people it suspects of terrorism. Its actions, including its shocking announcement last week of a new power of house arrest, have rightly been condemned as an attack on civil liberties. But cases of suspected terrorism are not the only ones in which the principles of the criminal justice system have been abandoned. The state has given itself new powers to deal with minor offences and other crimes which are scarcely less draconian than those to deal with suspected terrorism.

Over the past decade, anti-social behaviour – hellish neighbours, beggars, teenage gangs – has become a big worry in Britain. Rightly or wrongly, people think that drunkards and beggars are more aggressive these days, that teenagers are more threatening and that bad children have got worse. Explanations vary, with some blaming 1960s liberalism and others 1980s individualism. But all agree that the normal remedies for dealing with neighbourhood tyrants are not up to the task. The police lack the time to collect evidence; witnesses are too scared to testify; wrongdoing is difficult to prove; and sentences are too mild.

In response to such difficulties, the government has created a new set of legal tools. Chief among them is the anti-social behaviour order, or ASBO. This is a list of restrictions tailored to an individual offender that can now be obtained either in a civil hearing or following a criminal conviction.

Troublemakers as young as ten years old can be barred from entering neighbourhoods, ringing doorbells, using public transport and mobile phones or even uttering certain words for a minimum of two years. Securing an ASBO is easy. Hearsay evidence, for instance, is admissible in court. The consequences of stepping out of line are weighty: a maximum of five years in prison for doing something that is not necessarily an offence in law. Not surprisingly, such a powerful weapon is popular: more than a thousand ASBOs were handed out in the first half of 2004.

That delights MPs, who were sick of hearing stories from their constituents about local teenagers who have terrorised the neighbourhood by blasting music, breaking windows and spitting at passers-by. Prosecutors and the police are also pleased. Their powers to deal with low-level offences used to be weak. Now they are so draconian that they undermine the principles on which the criminal justice system is built.

The power to obtain anti-social behaviour orders was granted to the police and local authorities on the assumption that they were to be used with restraint. Just as the government promises to subject only genuinely scary terrorists to house arrest, so the forces of law and order are supposed to aim their most potent weapon only at the most dedicated and egregious troublemakers. Don't worry, goes the typically British assurance: our powers may be draconian, but decency and common sense will ensure we don't overuse them.

That's not what has happened. Obtaining an ASBO is so easy (fewer than one in 70 applications are turned down) that they have been used to tackle a wide range of undesirable behaviour. ASBOs allow the police to nail people for offences too minor to be criminal. Orders have been secured against crotchety old neighbours, prostitutes, beggars and mothers who argue with their children. Some of these people have subsequently been jailed for breaching their ASBOs: most absurdly, one man was sentenced to four months in prison for howling like a werewolf.

More worryingly, ASBOs allow the police to bypass the normal procedures of criminal justice when they suspect somebody of serious criminal activity but can't prove it. A suspected drug dealer, for instance, can be banned from using a mobile phone – a crucial tool, in his supposed profession. When he is caught doing so, he can be jailed.

It is not surprising that ASBOs are being used so frequently and so unwisely. After all, the English legal system is founded not on the assumption that everybody will behave with decency and restraint but on the rather more reliable conviction that most people, including the police, are capable of lying and may do so if it is to their advantage. Faced with two competing accounts of what one person has done to another, the courts normally give both of them a hard time. Accusations are minutely examined; witnesses are accused of fabricating their stories. Fail to make your case[1] and you lose.

As the police point out in defence of their enthusiasm for ASBOs, the criminal justice system does not always work well. If the police catch villains, prosecutors sometimes don't charge them; if they charge them, witnesses don't turn up to give evidence; if witnesses do turn up, the case is all too often adjourned because the courts' administration is chaotic. These are, indeed, serious problems; but the government needs to deal with them, not create new, lazy ways around them. The safeguards built into the criminal justice system are there for a good reason. If the police think a man is a drug dealer but can't prove it, he shouldn't go to jail, however often he uses his mobile phone.

The defence of civil liberties is rarely a vote-winner. People are, understandably, moved more easily by violence against people than by attacks on systems. Politicians are keener to be seen to be protecting victims than defending the rights of suspects. In a country without a written constitution, the rules that underlie a properly-run society are particularly vulnerable to the whims of populist politicians, and vigilance is therefore especially important.

Britons are lucky people, and complacent ones. The liberties they take for granted have evolved over a thousand years or so. The idea that any one government should seriously undermine them seems implausible. It isn't

From: *The Economist,* February 5th 2005

1 to make your case: *here:* to present your arguments in a convincing way

**Worksheet:**

maximum number of points attainable

**I. Questions on the text**

Read all the questions first, then answer them in the given order. Use your own words as far as is appropriate.

1. Explain how ASBOs work and describe the kinds of 'offences' that may lead to an ASBO. Do not make a list of individual examples but categorise your findings instead. 20
2. Why have ASBOs been welcomed in British society? 20

3. Analyse what goes wrong with the ASBOs. Include the recurrent example of the suspected drug dealer in your answer. 20
4. Why does the writer use the example of terrorism to introduce an article on ASBOs? How does the headline comment on both of these aspects? 20
5. What type of text is this and what kind of reader is it intended for? Justify your answer. 10
6. "Britons are lucky people, and complacent ones." (l. 73) Explain the sentence in its context. Show that it reflects the writer's main intention. 10

## II. Composition

Choose *one* of the following topics. Write about 250 to 300 words. 50

1. "Big Brother is watching us." – Is our privacy endangered by permanent surveillance?
2. Fighting crime means fighting the reasons for crime. Discuss.
3. Crime doesn't pay. Show how this theme is dealt with in a literary work by an English-speaking writer.
4. Imagine you are an English lawyer who represents somebody who is about to be sent to prison for breach of his ASBO. Write a convincing final speech for your client in court summing up the case and pleading clemency.

## III. Translation

Translate the following text into German: 50

200

Tony Blair talks incessantly about respect, yet there are few who have done more to degrade authority's respect for the public. Nowhere is that better seen than in the behaviour of the police, which gradually becomes more coercive and imbued with the idea that we are all bad hats until we prove otherwise. We now live in a country where anyone can be arrested for the slightest offence and compelled to become part of the government's DNA database.

We live in a country where young boys are taken aside and questioned for trying to knock conkers out of chestnut trees on public ground. Where a grandmother whose neighbour accused her of not returning a ball kicked into her garden was arrested and required to give her DNA.

What runs through all this seems to be a rather surprising dislike of the British people. The prevailing account[1] of Britain in the current political establishment has become deeply pessimistic and, to my mind, wrong. Yes, we have problems with home-grown terrorism, a swelling underclass, unintegrating minorities, but there is another story. Britain is also a success and it should occur to one of our political leaders to compliment the nation on its adaptability and deep reserves of virtue.

From *The Observer,* October 29th 2006

Anmerkung
1 account: *here:* image

## Lösungsvorschlag

### I. Questions on the text

1. *After you have read the text for the first time, you will immediately have the impression that the information which answers most of the questions is scattered all over the text rather than being limited to certain lines or paragraphs. So you had better make a list of all your findings before writing down your answer.*

   ASBOs are special orders aimed at individual people telling them to stop certain, very often common forms of behaviour which are thought to be offensive or even criminal. These can include
   - rude or strange behaviour: "crotchety" neighbours (l. 44); "howling like a werewolf" (l. 47)
   - aggressive behaviour: teenage gangs (l. 10); "breaking windows" (l. 30)
   - molesting people: beggars (l. 10), drunkards (l. 11); prostitutes (l. 44)
   - suspected crime: drug dealers (l. 50 ff.)

   These ASBOs can be easily obtained from a court by the police or by local authorities: even though a "civil hearing or … a criminal conviction" (l. 20/21) are required, "hearsay evidence" (l.24) is accepted. They can be applied even to ten-year-old children (l. 22). If a suspect is found acting against his ASBO, he may be sent to prison for much as five years.

2. *Again, you will find the information at various places in the text.*

   ASBOs have been welcomed because in the past ten years Britons have become increasingly worried about the rise in undesirable or aggressive behaviour which makes people feel more and more insecure (l. 10 ff.). Consequently, MPs are delighted with ASBOs because they can now say that politicians are finally doing something about teenagers terrorising the neighbourhoods (l. 29 ff.). Most of all, prosecutors and the police are "pleased" (l. 31) because they can now deal with offences that were either hardly punished, or not at all, because their "powers to deal with low-level offences" (ll. 31/32) were not strong enough: among other problems, the police usually do not have time enough to investigate (l. 15); witnesses do not turn up in court because they are afraid of giving evidence (l. 16/l. 61); trials are often postponed because of "chaotic" administration (l. 63); and consequently, the punishment very often turns out to be too mild (ll. 16/17).

3. *The example of the drug dealer appears twice in the text (l. 50 ff.; l. 65 ff.).*

   The main criticism is summed up in the writer's statement that ASBOs "are being used so frequently and so unwisely" (ll. 52/53). Even though the government aimed the ASBOs only at the worst troublemakers (l. 38) and assumed that they were to be used with great care and "restraint" (l. 35), too many of them (more than a thousand … in the first half of 2004; l. 28) were actually issued because they are so readily granted (fewer than 1 in 70 applications were turned down; ll. 41/42).
   The author also criticizes the fact that they are used "to bypass the normal procedures of criminal justice" (ll. 48/49). This is illustrated by the example of the suspected drug dealer: if the police can't nail him down for drug trafficking they now can issue an ASBO forbidding him to use his mobile phone. And if he is caught doing so he will be sent to prison for breaking this order rather than for his actual crime. The author thinks that this is a dangerous breach of English legal traditions because the government does not want to deal with the problems of the criminal justice system but rather wants to find "lazy" (l. 64), i.e. easy ways around them.

4. *Here you have two questions in one which you should answer separately.*

   The writer uses the example of terrorism as an eye-catcher because this is the more spectacular topic of the two. He accuses the British government of leaving behind "the principles of the criminal justice system" (l. 6) in the way it is dealing with terrorists even when they are only under suspicion. According to the author, the same violation of civil liberties can be seen in the way the government reacts to minor offences, which it feels cannot be prosecuted properly. The British government now deals with these as if they were terrorist actions.
   In the headline, he draws a parallel between these two types of offences. No matter if terrorists are put under house arrest or teenagers are banned from entering certain areas – in both cases the government feels entitled (it takes the liberty) to take away liberties from British citizens. But even in the case of terrorists, the author says, it is a violation of basic civil rights if they are taken away from someone who is only suspected of a crime without legal proof.

5. *A very general question which leaves you a lot of choice for your answer.*

   The text is a non-fictional article taken from a very distinguished English magazine. It is mainly argumentative; almost like a leader or commentary, it voices its opinion in clear plain words ("shocking announcement", l. 4; "rightly condemned", l. 5), illustrates the gravity of the problem with a great number of – sometimes strikingly absurd – examples. It is probably intended to rouse the attention of an educated, politically interested reader who may not be aware of the fact that even his own liberty might be at stake.

6. *The key words here are "lucky" and "complacent". So, comment on both of them – and don't confuse "lucky" and "happy"!*

   The writer thinks that Britons are lucky because they happen to live in a country with a very long democratic tradition where they benefit from a legal system that has guaranteed them civil liberties for centuries (l. 74). Today, most people in Britain take these liberties for granted because they have not had to fight for them as their ancestors had. Since the criminal justice system might not be perfect, safeguards (l. 64) are necessary and need to be protected.
   The writer accuses many Britons of being too complacent, i.e. of trusting politicians too readily; they rely too quickly on typically British ideas like "decency and common sense" (l. 39). He wants to convince his readers that any citizen, even a suspect, has rights which need to be defended. He warns them not to sit back thinking that nothing and no government can take away their freedom.

## II. Composition

1. In the film "The Truman Show" a young man finds out that his whole life has actually been filmed and broadcast nationwide without him having the slightest idea. The success of the film certainly does not owe itself to a clever script or a good cast alone but also to the fact that it plays with the fears and misgivings of many people.
   Certainly, one's life can seem to be completely transparent: personal data are being collected whenever we open a bank account, apply for part-time jobs, travel by plane, use the Internet or the telephone. We see video cameras being installed in public places – for our own and everybody else's security (as the authorities tell us). All our moves and steps, all our actions can be supervised and recorded – and later it can be tracked down where we were, who was with us, and what we did.

On the other hand: the fact that security checks before flights are so meticulously carried out by security personnel checking even sponge bags or pill boxes actually fills me with a sense of confidence. Not only women might actually find some relief in the fact that underground stations or car parks are supervised by cameras 24 hours. Moreover, today so much data is being collected that things are becoming a bit confusing even for the most ardent data collectors.
Many sceptical people are probably much more haunted by a vague fear rather than a concrete danger that our privacy is becoming endangered, an idea which is certainly cherished and nourished by certain politicians' wishful thinking. But, I still find lots of places where I can feel completely on my own. And at home, the only threat to my privacy are my parents (or perhaps my little brother) – and that is something I can deal with pretty well still.

2. Not only in Britain do people have the feeling that crime has increasingly become a problem for our society. And, of course, politicians are looking for ways of curing this "desease", often suggesting very superficial methods.
Of course, as some kind of first aid, crime needs punishment. When young people actually start beating up innocent passers-by, when people no longer know the difference between some harmless joke and serious vandalism, when no respect is shown for public or private property, something has to be done to show those offenders and criminals their limits, and it has to be done immediately.
But in the end these measures only help for a time – they only cure the symptoms of a disease instead of healing its real causes. Why for example do young people become criminals? Very often it is the absence of a proper home and lack of education: young people are very often left to themselves, they have no real guidance, get no emotional warmth, they feel that they don't belong. And if you have little or no relationship whatsoever to the world around you, you might as well destroy it.
In other cases it is the absence of a perspective: if you feel you are at the lower end of society and that society has given up on you – why should you care about what others think of you? No one seems to care about what happens to you – why then should you bother about what happens to someone else?
So I think that society should invest more money and time for example on the education and employment of young people. It is money well spent because in the long run it will prevent people from becoming criminals … and society can spend less money on prisons, police and security measures.

3. *When looking for an example to illustrate the sentence "Crime does not pay" you might be tempted to choose Shakespeare's Macbeth. But the quotation is one of these commonplace remarks usually referring to the more recent genre of detective novels or films. So we leave this aspect of the play to Thurber and his Macbeth Murder Mystery and rather turn to something more down-to-earth like Graham Greene's The Third Man.*

Graham Greene's novel *The Third Man* centres around the mysterious character of Harry Lime, a man who has chosen to make a lot of money in post-war Vienna by diluting penicillin and selling it on the black market where huge prices are paid for this newly-invented remedy because it was in short supply. Harry does not have any scruples about the disastrous consequences his criminal activities have on the patients, he is only interested in the huge profits he can make – free of tax, as he cynic-ally remarks to his friend Rollo Martins.
The story is set at the moment when Harry Lime's luck is already beginning to run out: the British Military police have tracked him down. Harry, who started out as a pupil at an English boarding school with an engaging personality and a promising future, who

managed to lead a life of affluence amid a world struck by war, now has to live virtually underground hiding in the sewage system of the Austrian capital. All his money will not help him in the end when he is killed by his friend Rollo Martins whom he tried to bribe by offering him a share in his profits.
Like any writer of detective stories, Greene sticks to the principle that in the end crime really does not pay. But the author goes even further by showing the moral depravity of his protagonist; friendship (Rollo Martins) and love (Anna, Harry's lover) mean nothing to him, politically he sides with anyone of the four allies who offers him help: Harry's criminal activities have corrupted his personality completely.
Thus, Greene shows that crime does not pay in any respect: Harry loses his money, his life and his moral integrity (if ever he had any). At the end, when he is shot like a rat in the Viennese underground, he has actually hit the bottom.

4. *Before you write this speech make sure you have got an interesting case for an ASBO. And if you feel familiar with the English legal system – even if only through films or books – this topic can be a real winner!*

Ladies and gentlemen,

Six months ago we met here in court for the first time when you issued an ASBO against my client forbidding her to put out food in her garden for the cats of her neighbourhood. Now, she has been charged with continuing to do so, according to information received from the next-door neighbours. They claim that my client puts out two bowls of cat's food every morning and every evening, and that up to twenty cats have been counted feeding there. Furthermore, they say that these cats ruin their gardens, disturb the peace and quiet with their noise, kill the bird life, and the leftover food attracts rats and mice.
Now, first of all let me say that all these accusations are only based on hearsay information. Do we really want to believe those accusations? I not only doubt the number of cats because we all know that these animals are loners, leading a very solitary life. I am also not convinced about the rats and the mice: how can any of them survive with such a number of feline enemies around?
But be it so – my client does not deny putting out food for some stray cats now and then, although this is clearly a breach of her ASBO. But then, she's not a criminal, her behaviour is in no way anti-social because it is not directed at any human being. She is a harmless elderly lady, living on a modest pension, paying her taxes, keeping her house and garden neat and tidy – you can't send her to prison. And that innocent charitable act of feeding some forlorn hungry cat – you can't call that a crime.
So I ask you to drop charges and let my client walk home free.

## III. Translation

Tony Blair spricht unablässig über gegenseitigen[1] Respekt, und dennoch gibt es nur wenige, die mehr dafür getan haben, die Achtung der Obrigkeit[2] für die Öffentlichkeit herabzusetzen. Nirgends kann man das besser sehen als im Verhalten der Polizei, die zunehmend immer aggressiver vorgeht[3] und von der Vorstellung durchdrungen ist, dass wir alle böse Finger[4] sind. Wir leben heute in einem Lande, in dem jedermann für das kleinste Vergehen festgenommen und verpflichtet werden kann, seine DNS[5] in der Datenbank der Regierung abspeichern zu lassen[1].
Wir leben in einem Land, in dem kleine Jungen beiseite genommen und verhört werden, weil sie versuchten, Kastanien von Bäumen[6] auf öffentlichem Grund herunter zu schlagen[7]. Wo eine Großmutter festgenommen wurde und eine DNS[5]-Probe abgeben musste[8], weil ihr Nachbar sie beschuldigte, einen Ball, der in ihren Garten geflogen[9] war, nicht wieder herausgegeben zu haben.

Was sich durch all das hindurch zieht, scheint eine ziemlich überraschende Abneigung gegenüber dem britischen Volk zu sein. Das vorherrschende Bild Großbritanniens bei seiner gegenwärtigen politischen Führung[10] ist zutiefst pessimistisch geworden, was meiner Meinung nach falsch ist[1]. Ja, wir haben Probleme mit hausgemachtem Terrorismus, mit einer anwachsenden Unterschicht, mit Minderheiten, die sich nicht integrieren wollen[11], aber es gibt auch eine andere Seite[1]. Großbritannien ist doch auch eine Erfolgsgeschichte[1], und es sollte einem unserer politischen Führer endlich mal[1] in den Sinn kommen, dem Land für seine Anpassungsfähigkeit und die tiefreichenden Tugendreserven ein Kompliment zu machen[12].

Anmerkungen

1 stilistisch bedingte Änderungen bzw. Einfügungen
2 *authority:* Behörden geht ebenfalls
3 *coercive:* Adjektiv aufgelöst; andere Übersetzungsmöglichkeit: z. B. „zu Zwangsmitteln (zu Nötigung) greifen“
4 in dem Ausdruck „böser Finger“ ist zumindest das Englische *bad* enthalten
5 „DNA“ ist auch möglich
6 Im Deutschen ist die Wiederholung von „Kastanien“ bei „Bäumen“ unsinnig
7 *knock:* es gibt viele Methoden: man kann sie „herunterschlagen“, „herunterwerfen“, „herunterholen“
8 *require* hat hier diesen allgemeinen Sinn des Hilfsverbs
9 *kicked:* der Ball kann auch „geschossen“, „gekickt“ worden sein
10 hier ist das Fremdwort „Establishment“ durchaus die gleich gute Wahl
11 beachte die *-ing*-Form!
12 „loben“ gibt den Sinn auch wieder

## Leistungskurs Englisch 2007
## Textaufgabe II

**Turning Thirty**

I walked into the pub off the Gray's Inn Road[1] and saw him slouching at the bar, and it was as if no time had passed.

The pub was one where we'd often met, and which I'd not visited since. I went in there today because I wanted a drink. It wasn't nostalgia or anything; to tell the truth, I'd hardly taken in where I was. The pub just happened to be the one I was passing at the moment I realized I really could not face the tube just then without a little lubricant.

With the end of our affair, we'd ceased to see each other. It wasn't something that had to be arranged: we had never moved in the same circles, and our one mutual acquaintance had moved to America soon after she'd introduced us.

Now at the sight, so familiar five years ago but not since, of my one and only adulterous lover, I came unanchored in time. I felt a little jolt, as if I'd seen a ghost, and then I shivered as that old sado-masochistic cocktail of lust and anger and loneliness began to spread throughout my system, and I went up to him with a sort of casual, sort of wicked grin, the way I used to, as if we'd planned this meeting and I was pretending we hadn't.

We drank; we flirted; we fought. And all of a sudden the barman was calling time. That couldn't be right. But the clock on the wall said it was, and I looked around and realized we were the only customers left.

We walked all the way down to Holborn[1] tube station, hand in hand, like innocent lovers. The hour and the darkness gave us that freedom.

"You're driving me crazy," he said, low-voiced. "This is no good. I want to make love to you. Come back with me."

"To Kent? Your wife won't mind?"

"I'm on expenses. We can get a hotel room. I said I might have to stay overnight … In fact, I do; I've missed the last train."

All our lovemaking had been in dark corners or in cheap hotels. We'd only spent the whole night together twice. I'd planned and chosen nights Peter was away, but Nick had had to call home, once from a pay phone in a station, once from the hotel room.

I wanted sex with him, violent and annihilating, but I couldn't deal with the emotions of before and after.

"I can't," I said abruptly, pushing him off, fixing my clothes. "I haven't missed my train and I'm not going to." I began walking towards the station.

"I'm sorry," he said humbly. Although we'd both been married, both, therefore, equally guilty, I'd reserved the role of the innocent. Of course, the husband I betrayed had already betrayed me, but I didn't tell Nick that. From his readiness to shoulder all the guilt I guessed that I was not the first woman his wife might have cause to hate. This, of course, added to the anger I felt at him and at faithless men everywhere.

"If you knew how much I've missed you – how much you still mean to me – can I see you again?"

"I don't think so," I said. "Nothing's changed. Has it?"

He looked very sad. "I guess not."

I had a ticket, he didn't, so I pushed through the turnstile and left him without looking back. In my mind, though, I never stopped looking back. I had plenty of time to think, for it's a long journey from Holborn to South Harrow[2], with a long, cold wait on the platform at Acton Town[2] making it even longer at that time of night.

Tears came to my eyes and then dried up. Older recollections – highly charged sexual moments – mingled with the memories of a few hours before. Things he'd said to me, things we'd done. Even more powerfully: all the things we hadn't done.

I was fairly drunk. Feeling no pain, as they say – except in my heart. As I walked up the hill from South Harrow station I cursed myself for not having gone with him, for not having seized a precious few hours of joy. Why did I always worry about what came next, why was I so desperate never to be caught out, always to behave correctly? What was the big deal about faithfulness and propriety, and getting home before dawn? It had never made me happy.

All too soon I was standing on the doorstep, trying to dig out my key from the clutter in the bottom of my handbag. I couldn't find it, but that didn't mean a choice between dumping everything out on the ground or ringing the bell – long ago, and without telling Peter, I had hidden a spare as insurance. The brick was still loose and the key was still there. It was a bit stiff turning in the lock, but it let me in.

The house was dark and silent. He hadn't even left a light on for me. I felt annoyed and yet relieved that I wouldn't have to hide my guilt and lie. With luck, I wouldn't wake him. I switched on the light in the corridor and opened the bedroom door and then I stared in horror feeling everything, my own sense of identity, swirling madly.

The bedroom furniture had changed. The bed was in a different position. And in the bed, sleeping beside Peter, was a woman. Peter's wife.

Not me – I wasn't Peter's wife any longer. I wasn't anything to Peter. Not since our divorce had become final, more than two years ago. And for two years before that we had ceased to live as man and wife.

I stared and stared as if seeing a ghost, but the only ghost in that house was me, the ghost of myself as I had been five years ago, when I was turning thirty. Meeting Nick tonight had brought that troubled young woman back to life, made her more real than the woman I thought I was now, thirty-five and single, living in a shared flat in Kilburn[2], with a room and a life of her own. What sort of life was it that could vanish so completely after a brief meeting with an old lover?

From: Lisa Tuttle, *Turning Thirty*, in: *The Time Out Book of London, Short Stories*, Penguin 1993

1 Gray's Inn Road, Holborn: places in central London

2 South Harrow, Acton Town, Kilburn: London suburbs

**Worksheet:**

maximum number of points attainable

## I. Questions on the text

Read all the questions first, then answer them in the given order. Use your own words as far as is appropriate.

1. Describe how and where the meeting between the narrator and Nick comes about. — 10
2. Sum up the information the text contains about their relationship up to the meeting in the pub. — 10
3. Do the couple's words and actions that night confirm the narrator's impression that "no time had passed" (l. 2) since their affair? Give evidence from the text. — 20
4. Examine the narrator's feelings and reflections after she has left Nick. Why does she refuse to have sex with him, and how does she herself feel about her decision later? — 20
5. What is the surprise at the end of the story? Analyse as precisely as you can how the writer prepares us for it and how we and the narrator are disillusioned step by step. — 20
6. What do the ending and the title reveal about the narrator's state of mind and her situation in life? — 10
7. How does the narrative technique affect the reader's perception of the story? Show that the narrative perspective is important for the surprise ending. — 10

## II. Composition

Choose *one* of the following topics. Write about 250 to 300 words. — 50

1. Do gender roles as presented in British and/or American media reflect reality in modern society?
2. Faithfulness – a concept of the past?
3. The power of passion in literature. Choose one work by an English-speaking writer and say why it has impressed you.
4. You have been asked to contribute an article for the student magazine *Happy Scholar* on different aspects of life in a shared flat. Speaking from your own experience advise a newcomer on the advantages and disadvantages.

## III. Translation

Translate the following text into German: — 50

200

Culturally unique to the UK, pubs[1] are the sociable drinking establishments that often act as the focal point of the community particularly in villages and small towns.
The drinking of alcohol in pubs has a long history in the UK, dating back to Roman England when inns were opened for weary travellers to buy refreshments during their long journeys. By the time the Romans left, the beginnings of the modern pub had been firmly established. During the early Middle Ages the demand for inns began to grow as pilgrimages and travel became more po-

pular. In 1393 King Richard II passed a law stating that all landlords must erect signs outside their pubs, or else risk losing their right to sell ale. This was how the 'pub sign' came into being with most pub signs containing pictures rather than words because most pub patrons were illiterate. Today, many British pubs still have decorative signs hanging over their doors.
The mid 19th century saw restrictions being placed on the opening hours of licensed premises. However, the Licensing Act[2] 2003 has allowed pubs to apply to the local authority for opening hours of their choice. It is worth noting here, though, that licensing laws in Scotland differ from the rest of the UK, and pubs there generally have more flexible opening hours.

From: http://www.lookupapub.co.uk/uk_pub_guide.asp

Anmerkungen
1 pub(s): nicht übersetzen
2 Licensing Act: nicht übersetzen

---

## Lösungsvorschlag

### I. Questions on the text

1. On her way home in London the narrator feels like having a drink and, for the first time since their separation five years ago, enters the pub where she and Nick used to meet and finds him already there. Supposedly she has not chosen this particular place on purpose.

2. *The relevant information is to be found in lines 10 to 13, 25 to 27 and 65.*

   Their affair had been an adulterous one. She describes it as sexually charged and, on her side, mixed with strong emotions of "anger and loneliness" (l. 12). Usually they had arranged their secret meetings in all but romantic places and had had to lie to their spouses (l. 25 ff.). Only twice had they been able to spend the night together. It had been her first and only extramarital relationship, and she suspects Nick, who still is married to his wife, of having had other lovers before (l. 33 ff.). Her own marriage has ended in divorce (l. 65 f.).

3. Most of what the narrator tells and what the lovers do and say during their meeting confirms this impression. When they chance upon each other in the pub apparently neither of them is really surprised – they immediately follow the patterns of their former relationship – "as if we'd planned this" (l. 14) – with all the usual ingredients of flirting, kissing and even fighting (l. 15) and the old "cocktail" (l. 12) of emotions. They hold hands "like innocent lovers" on their way to the tube station (l. 18). Both of them feel a powerful desire to make love (l. 20 ff.) and start discussing where they could do it.

4. *Notice that for a complete answer you need to cover three aspects: the narrator's feelings after leaving Nick, her reasons for rejecting him, and her feelings afterwards.*

   After leaving Nick the narrator is overcome with sadness and pain. She remembers the time when they were still lovers (ll. 45–48) and begins to regret that she refused to go with him: "I cursed myself" (l. 49).
   She refuses to have sex with him because she feels she could not cope with the emotions (l. 28 f.) connected with it. Her anger about his and other men's infidelity

(l. 36), and the fact that her reasons for breaking up are still valid (l. 39), contribute to her decision.
Afterwards she criticizes herself for being too strict about traditional values like "faithfulness and propriety" (l. 52), of worrying too much about the consequences instead of giving way to what she herself would have wanted, at least for "a precious few hours of joy" (l. 50).

5. *This question looks a bit complicated. It is best to describe the surprise ending first and then follow the narrator's and the reader's disillusionment at the same time. You will meet with difficulties in tracing the author's preparatory hints. In our opinion there are none – the end comes as a real surprise to us, which makes it all the more interesting. Don't just ignore this part of the question, however, but explain your doubts. We found only one reference to some kind of preparation, in the middle of the last part (see below).*

   It seems at first as if the narrator is returning to her marital home but, to the reader's surprise, it turns out that she has come to the wrong place: it is now the home of her ex-husband and his new wife.
   To the narrator and to us everything appears normal. She finds her spare key where she used to hide it. Her husband must have gone to bed, as no lights are turned on. From now on normality begins to crumble rapidly. When she opens the bedroom door, the narrator and we are shocked: the bed is not where it should be! On her next realization that there is a strange woman lying with Peter she and we ask ourselves whether her husband is doing what she refused to do an hour ago. When she comprehends that she is looking at Peter's wife, both narrator and reader are confused before understanding that it is she who is the intruder and has sneaked into Peter's and his new wife's bedroom.
   The writer does not really prepare us beforehand for the ending. Only when the narrator stares "in horror" at the scene and doubts her own identity (l. 62) do we begin to brace ourselves for a surprise.

6. *We recommend starting with the second part of the question as it takes up the narrator's thoughts following her surprise and shock.*

   The narrator is now 35 years old, single again, and shares a flat with others. The meeting with Nick has shaken her illusions about having come to terms with her divorce and her new life. She sees herself as a "ghost" of who she was, a "troubled young woman" (l. 68 ff.) who would readily turn back the clock to the life she had been leading before.
   The title refers to the assumption of many people that one reaches a turning point at thirty and to the fact that the narrator's life did suffer a break: when she turned thirty she ended her affair with Nick and her marriage, in exchange for something worse.

7. *For narrative techniques see "Tips for Questions on the Text" (perspective) and "Stichwortverzeichnis III (point of view"). Begin your answer with a brief description of the first-person's point of view, and continue with its effects on the reader.*

   The author uses a first-person point of view, by which the reader is invited to take for granted what the protagonist says and feels, and what he comments on situations and people. The problem here is that the narrator is not convincingly reliable – can we really accept that she is telling the truth, for example, when she claims to have chosen the pub by accident (l. 4)? Her limited perspective, however, makes the surprise ending more dramatic – the reader is as taken aback at the unravelling of reality as the narrator.

## II. Composition

1. *The topic leaves you the choice to use observations from different British and/or American papers, TV programmes, or films. You can either state your case with a variety of sources from different media or concentrate on one example with which you are well acquainted. Similarly, you can work on one or both genders. Maybe you should begin by making it clear to yourself what your actual view on gender roles is.*

   According to scientific research males and females have been found more alike than different. Yet there is a consensus that women have much too long been subjected to the clichés of the playmate and the housewife, serving men's 'superior' needs and making themselves agreeable to them. Modern society sees women as equal to men, as peers and partners, and tries to achieve more balanced gender roles. As the media are largely influential towards shaping public ideas and behaviour it is worth looking at their presentation of women, as an example.
   It is true that more and more women in films are shown in responsible positions. There is an increasing number of female police officers, judges, corporate executives and university professors portrayed on the screen.
   A look at the immensely popular American television series, 'Desperate Housewives', however, shows that women are not yet taken seriously enough. This show takes us back to a time when two-parent, middle-class families lived on single incomes and women's identities were basically determined by the men they married and the children they raised. Husbands were too important to trouble themselves with childcare or housework. Only one of the women, Susan, has a job, which, besides, is not made much of. Their main preoccupations seem to be how to make themselves more beautiful and sexually attractive to their spouses. If this does not work they become 'desperate' and neurotic. Between the lines appears the question whether they might have too much time and freedom. 'Desperate Housewives', which was, incidentally, written by a man and is watched by an only slightly smaller percentage of men than women, only conserves gender inequality and reinforces sexual stereotypes. If this is representative of the majority concept of gender roles, this programme reflects reality indeed – but I hope it is not.

2. *In our example we introduce the composition with a general observation which concludes with the repetition of the topical question. After making a few points we answer it with our personal opinion.*

   From the media we sometimes get the impression that open relationships, with their tolerance of unfaithfulness, are on the rise, especially among the rich and beautiful. In former times such a concept was unheard of and considered to be outrageous and destructive to society. Does this mean faithfulness is a thing of the past?
   It is common knowledge that partnerships only work with certain rules that have been agreed upon by all parties, whether by tradition or contract. In the past, a breach of fidelity in marriage, above all by the woman, was severely frowned upon and even punished by law. In the biblical commandments, adultery figures were seen as a most grievous sin. Yet the past lies behind us and the churches have lost much of their power so that faithfulness might have lost its moral imperative. It is doubtful, however, whether a committed relationship, even today, can be maintained without the foundation of mutual trust and loyalty. How can one continue to love one's partner, if they play around with others, giving the signal that you are easily replaceable? Cheating on each other is like cheating in a criminal way – and who wants to rely on a cheater?
   Even in close relationships people may have different ideas and perceptions about fidelity but I rather think the more faithful they are to each other the more stable will

be their ties. If you really want to preserve your marriage or your love, don't depend on your partner's tolerance! Faithfulness, to me, is neither a concept of the past nor of the present, it is only a question of character.

3. *Apart from trivial fiction, English literature is not exactly a treasure trove for tales of powerful passions. Only few of you will be familiar with the romantic masterpiece 'Wuthering Heights' by Emily Brontë, but some may have studied Romeo and Juliet or Othello. As we already wrote about the former in the 1998 Abitur solutions, we here chose the latter. Before you describe your impressions of the drama it is quite in order to summarize it briefly.*

   There is hardly a better example for the power of passion in literature than Shakespeare's Othello. In this tragedy the dramatist develops the predicament of the 'Moor of Venice', a middle-aged, highly respected general, who has secretly married Desdemona. She is the young daughter of a Venetian senator, who, much against his will, has to accept their union after all. Due to the machinations of the dissatisfied officer Iago, Othello is driven into insane jealousy and kills his innocent wife. When he becomes aware of his mistake, he takes his own life as well.
   Besides the drama's literary qualities, the beauty of its poetry and imagery, it demonstrates, through Shakespeare's masterful plotting and character development, what tragic consequences passion can lead to. The problem is that the protagonist is not sure of his own worth and whether he really deserves a wife like the beautiful, 'upper class' Desdemona. Thus he becomes an easy prey for Iago's insinuations about her alleged infidelity and the fake evidence of it convinces him too readily. Shakespeare shows how the emotion of boundless love turns into desperate jealousy and is eventually defeated by the dark side of passion: Othello strangles his loyal wife. It is particularly moving how Othello reacts to his crime, how he immediately feels the loss ('a huge eclipse of sun and moon'), and how he yearns for the fires of hell to punish him, when he realizes what he has done.

4. *To make it sound more like the article required in the task, rather than an argumentative composition, you might address the newcomer at the beginning and speak to him or her directly in the course of your text. It is advisable to make a list of pros and cons before you start.*

   A Word of Advice for the Homeless Newcomer

   You are new to this great university and have not found a place to live yet? Then read on and profit from the experienced opinion of one who has spent all his student days in shared flats and can truly make an informed judgment of its pleasures and pitfalls.
   Sharing a flat means living with people of similar age and interests. You will join a group who will be the first friends you make in your new surroundings. Returning to your digs after classes, you will feel like coming home to your family. Even if you are not too crazy about all your flat mates, there will always be some you get really close to. Also rates are definitely much more affordable than elsewhere. You may even reduce your expenses by preparing your own meals, or, even better, by cooking together – which is in itself a great social event. A shared flat offers community and privacy at the same time. You will always have people around you to talk to and to help you with your problems, and you can easily retire to your private room when you feel like it. You have the space and the use of communal areas such as living room, bathroom and kitchen, yet there is always the peace and quiet of your room, where you can mind your own business.
   Does this sound like paradise? Good, but before you rush off hunting for a shared flat take the time to look at some potential drawbacks.

If you are the typical lone ranger – desist! If not, choose well in any case. If the landlord's house rules are too prohibitive, look for another place! Take a good look at your prospective flat mates, too – maybe you hate smokers, vegetarians, or people with incompatible lifestyles? And, before I forget – be prepared for heated arguments like who has to clean the kitchen.
All things considered I dare say that sharing a flat is the most sociable and cheapest way to live, at least for freshmen – with the chance of making life-long friends.

## III. Translation

Als eine kulturelle Besonderheit[1] des Vereinigten Königreichs sind Pubs Einrichtungen für das Trinken in Gesellschaft[2], welche oft den Mittelpunkt des Gemeinschaftslebens[3] darstellen, besonders in Dörfern und Kleinstädten.
Der Alkoholkonsum in Pubs hat eine lange Geschichte in Großbritannien[4] und geht zurück auf das römische England, als Schenken eröffnet wurden, damit müde Wanderer[5] auf ihren langen Reisen Erfrischungen kaufen konnten. Bis zum Rückzug der Römer hatten sich die Anfänge des heutigen Pub fest etabliert.[6] Während des frühen Mittelalters begann die Nachfrage nach Gasthöfen mit der zunehmenden Beliebtheit[1] von Pilgerfahrten und Reisen zu wachsen. Im Jahre 1393 erließ König Richard II ein Gesetz, welches besagte, dass jeder Wirt[7] ein Schild vor seinem Pub aufstellen musste, andernfalls er riskierte, seine Lizenz zum Ausschank von Bier[8] zu verlieren. So entstand das ‚Pubschild', wobei die meisten Pubschilder eher Bilder als Worte enthielten, da die meisten Gäste[9] Analphabeten waren. Heute hängen immer noch kunstvoll gestaltete Pubschilder über den Türen vieler Pubs.
Um die Mitte des 19. Jahrhunderts wurden Einschränkungen für die Öffnungszeiten von Lokalen mit Schankerlaubnis verhängt.[10] Der Licensing Act von 2003 jedoch gestattet[11] es den Pubs, bei der Kommunalbehörde individuelle[12] Öffnungszeiten zu beantragen. Es ist hier jedoch erwähnenswert, dass die Schankgesetze in Schottland sich vom Rest des Vereinigten Königreichs unterscheiden – dort haben Pubs allgemein freiere Öffnungszeiten.

Anmerkungen

1 Ein Wechsel der Wortart (Adjektiv – Substantiv) ist oft eine gute Alternative zur wörtlichen Übersetzung.
2 Auch: „das gesellige Trinken"
3 Die Erweiterung eines Grundworts (hier mit „-leben") führt oft zu stilistisch besseren Übersetzungen
4 Hier zur Abwechslung einmal ein Ausdruck mit gleicher Bedeutung
5 „Reisende" und „Reisen" so kurz hintereinander klingt unelegant
6 Ein Aktivsatz hört sich oft besser an als ein Passivsatz
7 Es ist besser, wenn man hier *all landlords* mit „jeder Wirt" übersetzt und den Singular im gesamten Satz beibehält
8 *Ale* wäre eigentlich korrekter, wurde aber nicht zum Stehen lassen freigegeben. Immerhin wird der Begriff auch in England oft synonym für „Bier" gebraucht
9 Dass es Gäste von Pubs sind, versteht sich von selbst
10 Das *saw* lässt sich hier nicht adäquat wiedergeben
11 *has allowed:* wir verwenden hier das Präsens, da das Gesetz immer noch gilt und dies ein gutes Beispiel dafür ist, wie das present perfect auch mit dem deutschen Präsens übersetzt werden kann
12 Natürlich geht auch *flexible*. Gemeint ist jedoch sicher, dass jeder Wirt seine eigenen Öffnungszeiten beantragen, nicht aber, dass er sie flexibel handhaben kann.

**Dollywood Values**

No one goes hungry at Dollywood. The cake stands at Dolly Parton's[1] theme park in Tennessee sell slices of apple pie that weigh three pounds each, and that's before you bury them in ice cream. The mixed appetisers at the best restaurant consist of a heap of battered[2]and deep-fried cauliflower florets[3], a mound of deep-fried cheese sticks and a pile of potatoes slathered in melted cheese. The next course might be a vast platter of southern-fried chicken. Only a real man still has room for apple pie after such a feast, but there are plenty of real men at Dollywood. And real women, too.

Dolly Parton's father was a semi-literate sharecropper, and she grew up in a one-room shack, with ten siblings and no indoor plumbing. Yet by the time she was in her late 20s, she was in a position to tell Elvis Presley to get stuffed. The King wanted to cover one of her songs, "I Will Always Love You". His agent demanded the usual terms, which included signing over half the rights to the tune itself. Ms Parton said no; a bold snub that made her millions. Her composition was a global smash. Whitney Houston's cover alone sold more than 10m copies. Saddam Hussein used an Arabic version as a campaign song in 2002, though it would be unfair to blame Ms Parton for his victory, since there was no one else on the ballot.

Having made a fortune from music and occasional movies, Ms Parton has ploughed a chunk of it back into the land where she grew up, near Pigeon Forge in the Great Smoky Mountains. The central attraction is Dollywood, which lures some 2m visitors a year. That is hardly world-beating – the Magic Kingdom at Walt Disney World had nearly 17m visitors last year. But Dollywood is a different kind of enterprise.

The theme-park industry has two tiers. The really big money is in what insiders call "destination" parks. These are so fancy and expensive that people fly thousands of miles to visit them. Asian governments invite Disney and Universal Studios to build ever-bigger parks on their territory in the hope that this will spark a tourist boom, which it usually does. Because they aim for a global audience, Hollywood theme parks tend to be spectacular but self-consciously inoffensive to all nationalities. To learn about the real America, you have to look at its smaller theme parks – the ones only Americans visit.

People do not fly to Dollywood; they drive there in big cars full of squabbling children. East-coast accents, let alone foreign ones, are rare. The park is thus an excellent window on what people in this part of the American heartland like. One thing they appear to like a lot is their country. The Liberty gift shop sells a staggering array of patriotic paraphernalia. You can buy a stars-and-stripes-decorated statuette of the Liberty Bell[4] with an eagle perched on it. There are CDs of Ms Parton, also in red, white and blue, singing "God bless the USA", and "My mom is a soldier" photo frames for kids whose mothers are in Iraq. The park even has a sanctuary for bald eagles injured in the wild.

Another thing visitors to Dollywood feel strongly about is God. The park has a chapel, named after the doctor and part-time preacher who delivered baby Dolly for a bag of cornmeal. A bookshop manned by trainee preachers sells Bibles and Christian-themed novels. Employees at Dollywood are "not discouraged" from sharing their faith with customers, says a guide. And there is no alcohol on sale.

Lastly, the folks at Dollywood like to celebrate their own folk culture and music. Parts of the park look like a 19th-century Appalachian town. You can watch real artisans blowing glass, making lye soap[5] and carving chairs the old-fashioned way. Some have developed a country sales banter. "No cameras," says Tom, who makes wooden wagons. "The law in Mississippi's still looking for me."

Indigenous music is everywhere. In one corner is the Smoky Mountain String Band – three guys in blue dungarees with a banjo, fiddle and upright bass. In another is a bluegrass band called Naomi and the Wood Brothers. In Europe, exhibitions of traditional music and crafts tend to be subsidised and unpopular. At Dollywood, they are neither.

Sophisticates sneer at Ms Parton's theme park. The *Daily Express,* a British paper owned by a man who also peddles pornography, calls it "tacky". But the values it represents are as American as a three pound slice of apple pie. Dollywood's calorific abundance is quite healthy compared with Hershey Chocolate World in Pennsylvania. Its patriotism seems restrained next to the nearby Patriot Park, with its annual Patriot Festival. Its brand of Christianity is less in-your-face than, say, the Holy Land Experience in Florida. It is tolerant, too. Ms Parton has many gay fans, who hold unofficial get-togethers at her park. Her grandfather was a hellfire preacher, but Ms Parton has an empathy for sinners. As a girl, she thought the town hooker in her make-up and stilettos was the prettiest thing she had ever seen. "She was trash," Ms Parton tells interviewers, "And I thought: That's what I want to be when I grow up."

Most important, Dollywood offers a rags-to-riches tale with a simple happy ending. Ms Parton was born among the poorest whites in America. She had talent. She worked hard. She became fabulously rich and famous. The world's first cloned sheep was named after her (it was cloned from a mammary cell). Yet despite all the adulation, she is still married to the man she met outside a laundrette in Nashville 43 years ago, when she was 18. And her husband is such a down-to-earth fellow that he shuns the limelight entirely. If reporters arrive at the couple's front gate while he is in the garden and want to talk to him, he pretends to be the gardener. That may be too corny for Hollywood, but it resonates in the Great Smoky Mountains.

From: *The Economist,* November 10th 2007

1 Dolly Parton: famous country music singer also known for the size of her bosom

2 battered: covered in a mixture of milk, flour and egg

3 florets: small flower-like parts of a vegetable

4 Liberty Bell: American bell of great historic significance; symbol associated with the American Revolutionary War

5 lye soap: traditional form of soap

**Worksheet: Dollywood Values**

maximum number of points attainable

## I. Questions on the text

Read all the questions first, then answer them in the given order. Use your own words as far as is appropriate.

1. Describe Dolly Parton's background and her outstanding professional achievements. What makes her career a typical example of the American Dream? — 20
2. Show in detail that Dollywood represents typical, conservative American values. Give evidence from the text. — 20
3. Describe "what insiders call 'destination' parks" (ll. 22/23). To what extent do they differ from Dollywood? — 10

4. Analyse the writer's attitude towards Dollywood. How do language and tone express his view? 30
5. Examine Dolly's personality. Is it reflected in her park? 20

## II. Composition

Choose *one* of the following topics. Write about 250 to 300 words. 50

1. Can or should people be forced to adopt a healthy lifestyle?
2. Duty or pleasure?
   Write a speech with this title given by a student representative at an American or British graduation ceremony.
3. What are the values that constitute the essence of Western civilisation?
4. Comment on the cartoon.

Invading new markets    From: www.politicalcartoons.com

### III. Translation

Translate the following text into German: 50/200

During the research for this book, I was often asked what was the point in my writing about Englishness when the inexorable spread of American cultural imperialism would soon make this an issue of purely historical interest.

The economic influence of American corporate giants may indeed be overwhelming, and even pernicious, but their cultural impact is perhaps less significant than either they or their enemies would like to believe. Given increasing evidence of fragmentation of nations into smaller and smaller cultural units, it does not make sense to talk of a world of six billion people becoming a vast monoculture. The spread of globalization is undoubtedly bringing changes to the cultures it reaches, but change does not necessarily mean the abolition of traditional values.

Within Britain the fervour and power of Scottish and Welsh nationalists does not seem to be much affected by their taste for American soft drinks, junk food or films. Ethnic minorities in Britain are increasingly keen to maintain their distinctive cultural identities, and the English are becoming ever more fretful about their own cultural "identity crisis". In England, regionalism is escalating, and there is considerable resistance to the idea of being part of Europe, let alone part of any global monoculture.

From: Kate Fox, *Watching the English: the Hidden Rules of English Behaviour.*
London: Hodder & Stoughton 2004

## Lösungsvorschlag

### I. Questions on the text

1. *You will have to collect information from the whole text in order to answer this double question. So read the text carefully and take notes before writing down your answer!*

   Dolly Parton comes from a very modest background in the American heartland: she was born into a poor white family and was one of eleven children. Her father who could hardly read or write was a "sharecropper" (l. 8), i. e. he did not even own the land the family cultivated. The family home is called a "shack" (l. 9) which had only one room and no running water. In spite of all these hard conditions, Ms Parton used her musical talents, and by the time she was in her late 20s, she was already so famous as a singer and songwriter that even artists like Elvis Presley wanted to sing one of her songs. This tune – "I will always love you" – became such a huge success all over the world that it was even used in an Arabic version by former Iraq dictator Saddam Hussein. By the 1990s she had become so famous that the first cloned sheep in England was given her name. The author calls the story of her life "a rags-to-riches tale" (l. 62), the typical embodiment of the American Dream: someone from the most humble beginnings ("born among the poorest whites in America"; l. 63) uses his or her talent, works hard and becomes "fabulously rich and famous" (l. 64). She accumulated such a lot of money that she was even able to create her own theme park in her home in the Great Smoky Mountains of Tennessee, and gave it her name: Dollywood.

2. The text emphasizes three typical American values which are represented in Dollywood: patriotism, religion and folk culture. Among the patriotic items in the park, the text lists "statuettes of the Liberty Bell" (l. 33) decorated with the American flag or "CDs of Ms Parton" (l. 34) in America's national colours red, white and blue. Even America's national bird, the bald eagle, finds a "sanctuary" (l. 36) there when "injured in the wild".
   Another feature of Dollywood is the Christian religion. In the park grounds, visitors can go to a chapel; and there is also a bookshop whose staff consists of "trainee preachers" (l. 39) and which sells Bibles and books focusing on Christian topics. Consequently, no alcoholic drinks are sold in the park.
   Thirdly, American folk culture and music are celebrated everywhere in Dollywood. On the one hand, life in the Appalachians of the 19$^{th}$ century is re-created in some parts: visitors can watch "artisans blowing glass, making lye soap" (ll. 43/44) and other handicrafts of pioneer days. And elsewhere bands, with their traditional instruments and wearing their traditional outfits, can be heard playing the typical country and bluegrass music of the area.

3. "Destination" parks are parks like Disney World or Universal Studios: they are huge and attract millions and millions of visitors from all over the USA and even from all over the world. People fly there and are prepared to spend lots of money. They have become such a great success that they are imported into countries outside the USA. In order to attract such large audiences, they have to be neutral in their appeal, i.e. they must not feature anything of only regional or patriotic interest but must be "global" (l. 26).
   In contrast, parks like Dollywood tend to attract local audiences who drive there for the day in their "cars full of squabbling children" (l. 29). The number of visitors is accordingly much smaller, but they want to see their own familiar culture and values represented there. In the author's words, these smaller parks show "what people in this part of the American heartland like" (l. 31).

4. *As far as we know, this is the first time ever that you could attain 30 points for one single question!*

   Basically, one can say that the writer's attitude is ambivalent.
   On the one hand, he criticizes several aspects of Dollywood: he begins his text with a description of the food offered there, which seems to confirm all European clichés. He exaggerates by using hyperboles like "heap", "mound", "pile" or "vast" to describe the size of its portions; that it is unhealthy is emphasized by stating the ways in which it is prepared: it is "battered and deep-fried" or potatoes are "slathered in melted cheese". The writer becomes ironical when he calls the people who can eat such enormous portions "real men and women" – "real" meaning here "obese" (all quotations taken from the first paragraph). The author's irony is also present, when he applies the word "value" to something as prosaic as a "three pound slice of apple pie" (l. 53).
   When writing about typical, conservative American values represented at the park, the author distances himself from its visitors by employing a slightly patronising tone: "One thing they appear to like a lot is their country." (ll. 31/32); he calls the visitors "folks" who "celebrate their own folk culture and music" (l. 42) or who "feel strongly about … God" (l. 37). The enumeration of items that seem odd to Europeans – from "a stars-and-stripes-decorated statuette of the Liberty Bell" over "a bookshop manned by trainee preachers" to the performance of "indigenous music" – make the park and its visitors look provincial and simple. This attitude is also shown when using the metaphor "plough back into the land" (ll. 17/18) instead of "spend money on" thus referring to Ms Parton's rural, unintellectual background.
   In contrast to all its focus on the "real" America, the author now and then conveys the impression that all this is only fake, when he quotes a certain Tom "who makes wooden wagons" and who wants no pictures taken of him because "The law in Mississippi's still looking" for him (ll. 45/46).
   On the other hand, the text has a defensive and even somewhat admiring tone when writing about Dolly Parton and her achievements. For one, the writer defends it from criticism by "sophisticates". Next, he accuses the Daily Express of hypocrisy because its owner sells pornography. Furthermore he says that in comparison to other theme parks, Dollywood is neither as patriotic nor as openly religious, nor is its food as unhealthy as in other parks in the USA. In general, the author thinks that it is "an excellent window on what people in this part of the American heartland like" (ll. 30/31). By using this metaphor, he puts Dollywood and its visitors into a proper perspective and dimension – not to be seen and judged only by European eyes.

5. *Be careful: this question contains two parts; and there is more in the article on Dolly Parton's personality than on its reflection in her park!*

   First of all, Dolly Parton comes across as a hard-working, ambitious and very self-confident woman. Starting from very poor circumstances ("born among the poorest whites", l. 63), she managed to make a fortune by becoming a successful singer, songwriter, actress and businesswoman. On the other hand, she remained down-to-earth and did not forget her roots. So she "has ploughed a chunk of [her money] back into the land where she grew up" (ll. 17/18). She also wants to show the qualities of the American pioneers by displaying simple country life of the 19$^{th}$ century. Contrary to all those Hollywood celebrities, she seems to have had no affairs, but is "still married to the man she met … in Nashville 43 years ago, when she was 18" (ll. 65/66). She is known mainly as a country music singer – the music featured in her park. In her songs, she also shows her pride in being American – accordingly her patriotism is displayed in the park, too. She is obviously a Christian, which is also shown at Dollywood, but she is more tolerant than her grandfather ("a hellfire preacher"; l. 58): she does not only allow her gay fans to "hold unofficial meetings" at her park, but she also has a certain understanding ("empathy"; l. 58) for sinners. Lastly, Ms Parton has no intellectual ambitions – and she makes no secret of it: when she was a girl, she was impressed by the town hooker because – in Ms Parton's words – "she was trash" (l. 60). To which she unashamedly adds: "And I thought: That's what I want to be when I grow up" (ll. 60/61). And her park is what European intellectuals certainly would call "trash".

## II. Composition

1. Since the beginning of this year, a controversy has been going on in Germany about the prohibition of smoking in all public buildings including restaurants. Non-smokers and most politicians have welcomed the new legislation, whereas smokers and many proprietors of pubs and bars have protested against it. This is one recent example of the question whether people can or should be forced to adopt a healthy lifestyle.
When you first look at it, this seems a tempting idea: certain ways of living, certain habits are harmful to people – and they know it: scientists tell us that our health suffers badly. People, who eat too much, drink alcohol regularly, smoke or do sports like downhill skiing, risk injuries, high blood pressure, cancer etc. They become ill and they cost the taxpayer a lot of money, as well as the people who pay into health and life insurance. Those who watch their weight or do not drink or smoke have to pay for those who do not care about their personal health. Therefore, it seems only fair to force the latter to lead a healthy lifestyle.
On the other hand, this is easier said than done. Firstly, the question arises of how to control and supervise any of the regulations and measures that are needed to enforce these new laws. The failure to prohibit alcohol in the USA in the last century illustrates vividly that this proved impossible, even in a country where anti-alcoholism is deeply rooted in its history. Secondly, this would only lead to a general atmosphere of spying and ill will, which would consequently poison private and public life. Lastly, we cannot infringe everybody's fundamental right to choose their own lifestyle, their personal "pursuit of happiness".
To sum up, I think that private companies, e.g. life insurances have the right to impose certain restrictions on their customers, but when it comes to life in general, no government should be allowed to rule how people lead their life. Even if they waste it.

2. *The "pleistocean crustaceans" mentioned in the speech may be replaced by anything else you had to learn about at school even though you believed it was entirely useless. On page VIII of this book you will find a few tips for writing a speech. Note: contrary to popular belief, most teachers do not like flattery! So try to be honest and realistic!*

Mrs Kendall! Parents, teachers, fellow students!
This is a proud day for everyone here, but especially for all of us students. It is the day we have been looking forward to the last four years we have spent at Southbridge High: We have made it. And it is an appropriate moment to reflect upon.
Older people – and that includes parents – recalling their school days often refer to them as the best and happiest days of their lives. When I look back, I feel a strong tendency to disagree. A lot of my time at school was clouded by the word duty. The daily struggle to get up early, the fight against falling asleep in lessons, which sometimes were neither inspiring nor inspired, the hard work of doing my homework and preparing for tomorrow's lessons, when television or friends offered more exciting entertainment than the works of Shakespeare or Henry James. All this made the talk of school as days of pleasure seem rather ridiculous to me, especially, when my questioning the importance of pleistocean crustaceans was met by my teacher pointing out that "You might need to know about it someday". Life at school seemed nothing but a string, or rather a chain of duties.

On the other hand, school was not all misery and pain. I have made a lot of friends over the last years, and I am sure that some of those friendships will last forever. As for the teachers, I can honestly say they were no monsters, and some of them actually turned out to be devoted and caring. Thank you for putting up with my doubts. I would also like to say thank you to my parents who helped me through all the difficult times with their understanding and patience.

So, on reflection, it was not all that bad. And I am sure someday in the future I will look back on my school days and will be able to say, they were days of pleasure – not only of duty.

3. Reducing the question of what are the values that constitute the essence of Western civilization into an essay of about 300 words seems a rather frivolous undertaking to me. A simple enumeration of values alone would make up a list considerably longer, since there are so many of them: freedom of speech and all the other liberties, tolerance, access to education, equality in all its forms, respect for minorities, to mention only a few of the more idealistic ones – and there are others, more down-to-earth but equally important: choosing the partner you like, leading a life free from starvation etc. Now, as I am about to leave school and enter a new phase of my life, I may be allowed to concentrate on only one value that seems extremely important to me: freedom to lead an independent life.

   To me, one of the greatest achievements of our civilization is the idea that man – or woman – has the right to lead a life where he can choose his job, the place where he wants to live, his partner, his religious, political and philosophical beliefs and his personal lifestyle entirely on his own, and that no one, neither parents nor family, let alone governments or any other political or religious authority have any right to interfere. Advice is always heartily welcome, but no pressure should be put on anyone. I am aware that there are countries, which do not offer any of these rights, and there people lead happy lives, too, but personally I could never imagine becoming a contented person under such conditions.

   Life may be harder and more complicated, if the only guideline for judging what is good for you is your own personal choice, but I think this is one of the most essential values that we inherited from those brave men and women, who stood up against authorities and beliefs based only on tradition and habit. This is a heritage we must cherish and defend. Yes, it may make life more adventurous, but that makes it also more interesting.

4. *This cartoon contains such a lot of different details which make it difficult to describe with only 300 words unless you restrict yourself to the most important items.*

   The caption of the cartoon reads "Invading new markets" – that is its topic and that is what we see: a Third World country (perhaps a tropical island) is being invaded. The scene is reminiscent of the Normandy landings in 1944. But the invaders are no regular soldiers. Instead, they are figures taken from Walt Disney's comic world: the soldiers are Goofys commanded by Donald Duck and (in the foreground) a smiling Mickey Mouse with his gun. He and the soldiers are driving away a couple of natives, who are holding their arms above their heads in surrender. Instead of regular bombs and ammunition, the people are being attacked with television sets, dropped from airplanes and tins of coke, shot from a warship at sea. The uniforms and all the warships bear the logos of big American companies: Nike, Texaco, McDonald's etc. In the background a group of Goofy-soldiers are setting up a Microsoft flag, a scene similar to that famous picture of Iwo Jima.

   To my mind, the cartoon wants to express two things: first, modern invasions do not necessarily have to be fought with weapons, tanks, warships or soldiers. America's

wars today are mainly fought by her big companies, and the battlegrounds are the international markets. And secondly, America invades the world with her lifestyle and culture, which often serves as a vanguard.
To a point, I can agree with the cartoonist: the USA has swept the globe with her products, and her corporate giants do dominate the financial and economic world. But other industrialized countries are joining in – amongst them Germany. And American culture has had a huge influence since World War II, often wiping out a lot of traditional habits and customs. But obviously, there is something very appealing about American food, clothes, music or films because their success cannot be explained only by the use of force. So, it is fairly easy to attack America for her role as the only remaining world power. But we ourselves have readily helped, by allowing ourselves to be dazzled and seduced by what is being offered.

## III. Translation

*Hinweis: Der Text ist ein Paradebeispiel für die Frage, inwieweit Fremdwörter übersetzt werden sollen oder nicht, ein Problem, das gerade in solchen Prüfungen Schülern große Schwierigkeiten bereitet, auch wenn sie den Text verstehen: research; Englishness; cultural imperialism; economic; fragmentation; monoculture; globalization; traditional; soft drinks; junk food; cultural identities; cultural ‚identity crisis'; escalating; global monoculture … Hier hilft nur eine vorherige Diskussion und Klärung mit dem jeweiligen Korrektor …*

Während der Recherchen für dieses Buch wurde ich oft gefragt, was es denn überhaupt noch[1] für einen Sinn mache, über das Englischsein[2] zu schreiben in einer Zeit, in der die unaufhaltsame Ausbreitung des amerikanischen Kulturimperialismus dieses bald zu einer Angelegenheit von rein historischem Interesse machen würde.

Der wirtschaftliche Einfluss amerikanischer Riesenkonzerne mag in der Tat überwältigend und vielleicht sogar schädlich sein, aber ihre Auswirkung auf die Kultur ist vielleicht weniger bedeutend als sie oder ihre Feinde es gerne glauben möchten. Angesichts zunehmender[3] Beweise für die Zersplitterung von Staaten in immer kleinere kulturelle Einheiten macht es keinen Sinn davon zu reden, dass eine Welt von 6 Milliarden Menschen zu einer riesigen Einheitskultur[4] wird. Die Ausbreitung der Globalisierung bringt zweifellos Veränderungen in den Kulturen mit sich, die sie erreicht, aber Veränderung bedeutet nicht notwendigerweise die Abschaffung[5] traditioneller Werte.

Innerhalb Großbritanniens scheinen Feuereifer und Energie schottischer und walisischer Nationalisten kaum beeinträchtigt zu sein[6] von ihrer Vorliebe[7] für alkoholfreie Getränke, ungesundem Essen[8] und Filmen aus Amerika. Ethnische Minderheiten in Großbritannien sind zunehmend darauf bedacht, ihre unverwechselbaren kulturellen Eigenheiten zu bewahren, und die Engländer selber werden immer gereizter, was ihre eigene kulturelle Identitätskrise betrifft. In England greift die Regionalisierung immer weiter um sich und es gibt einen beträchtlichen Widerstand gegen die Vorstellung ein Teil Europas, geschweige denn ein Teil irgendeiner weltweiten Einheitskultur zu werden.

Anmerkungen
1 Stilistisch bedingte Einfügung
2 *Englishness*: es gibt viele Möglichkeiten diesen Begriff zu übersetzen, z. B. auch *englische Mentalität*
3 Auch möglich: immer zahlreicher werdender
4 Drastischer, aber auch richtig: kultureller Einheitsbrei
5 *Abolition*: auch Auflösung, Aufgabe; eine verbale Übersetzung mit *abschaffen, aufgeben* … ist auch geschickt
6 *To be*: hier auch zu werden
7 *Taste for*: auch verbal zu übersetzen mit *Geschmack finden an*
8 Natürlich könnte man auch die englischen Originalbegriffe *soft drinks* und *junk food* stehen lassen

## A Temporary Matter
by Jhumpa Lahiri

He ran his tongue over the tops of his teeth; he'd forgotten to brush them that morning. It wasn't the first time. He hadn't left the house at all that day, or the day before. The more Shoba stayed out, the more she began putting in extra hours at work and taking on additional projects, the more he wanted to stay in, not even leaving to get the mail or to buy fruit or wine at the stores by the trolley stop.

Six months ago, in September, Shukumar was at an academic conference in Baltimore when Shoba went into labor, three weeks before her due date. He hadn't wanted to go to the conference, but she had insisted; it was important to make contacts, and he would be entering the job market next year. She told him that she had his number at the hotel, and a copy of his schedule and flight numbers, and she had arranged with her friend Gillian for a ride to the hospital in the event of an emergency. When the cab pulled away that morning for the airport, Shoba stood waving good-bye in her robe, with one arm resting on the mound of her belly as if it were a perfectly natural part of her body.

Each time he thought of that moment, the last moment he saw Shoba pregnant, it was the cab he remembered most, a station wagon, painted red with blue lettering. It was cavernous compared to their own car. Although Shukumar was six feet tall, with hands too big ever to rest comfortably in the pockets of his jeans, he felt dwarfed in the back seat. As the cab sped down Beacon Street, he imagined a day when he and Shoba might need to buy a station wagon of their own, to cart their children back and forth from music lessons and dentist appointments. He imagined himself gripping the wheel, as Shoba turned around to hand the children juice boxes. Once, these images of parenthood had troubled Shukumar, adding to the anxiety that he was still a student at thirty-five. But that early autumn morning, the trees still heavy with bronze leaves, he welcomed the image for the first time.

A member of the staff had found him somehow among the identical convention rooms and handed him a stiff square of stationery. It was only a telephone number, but Shukumar knew it was the hospital. When he returned to Boston it was over. The baby had been born dead. Shoba was lying on a bed, asleep, in a private room so small there was barely enough space to stand beside her, in a wing of the hospital they hadn't been to on the tour for expectant parents. Her placenta had weakened and she'd had a cesarean, though not quickly enough. The doctor explained that these things happen. He smiled in the kindest way it was possible to smile at people known only professionally. Shoba would be back on her feet in a few weeks. There was nothing to indicate that she would not be able to have children in the future.

These days Shoba was always gone by the time Shukumar woke up. He would open his eyes and see the long black hairs she shed on her pillow and think of her, dressed, sipping her third cup of coffee already, in her office downtown, where she searched for typographical errors in textbooks and marked them, in a code she had once explained to him, with an assortment of colored pencils. She would do the same for his dissertation, she promised, when it was ready. He envied her the specificity of her task, so unlike the elusive nature of his. He was a mediocre student who had a facility for absorbing details without curiosity. Until September he had been diligent if not dedicated, summarizing chapters, outlining arguments on pads of yellow lined paper. But now he would lie in their bed until he grew bored, gazing at his side of the closet which Shoba always left partly open, at the row of the tweed jackets and corduroy trousers he would not have to choose from to teach his classes that semester. After the baby died it was too late to withdraw from his teaching duties. But his adviser had arranged things so that he had the spring semester to himself. Shukumar was in his sixth year of graduate school. "That and the summer should give you a good push," his adviser had said. "You should be able to wrap things up by next September."

But nothing was pushing Shukumar. Instead he thought of how he and Shoba had become experts at avoiding each other in their three-bedroom house, spending as much time on separate floors as possible. He thought of how he no longer looked forward to weekends, when she sat for hours on the sofa with her colored pencils and her files, so that he feared that putting on a record in his own house might be rude. He thought of how long it had been since she looked into his eyes and smiled, or whispered his name on those rare occasions they still reached for each other's bodies before sleeping.

In the beginning he had believed that it would pass, that he and Shoba would get through it all somehow. She was only thirty-three. She was strong, on her feet again. But it wasn't a consolation. It was often nearly lunchtime when Shukumar would finally pull himself out of bed and head downstairs to the coffeepot, pouring out the extra bit Shoba left for him, along with an empty mug, on the countertop.



**Worksheet: Lahiri, "A Temporary Matter"**

maximum number of points attainable

## I. Questions on the text

Read all the questions first, then answer them in the given order. Use your own words as far as is appropriate.

1. Sum up what happened in September and examine Shukumar's role in these events: does the text imply that he neglected his wife? — 20
2. Analyse the ideas and feelings about future parenthood that the cab ride stirs in Shukumar's mind. — 10
3. Compare Shukumar's and Shoba's attitude towards work before and after the events of last September. — 20
4. How have these events changed their relationship and their daily lives? — 20
5. How does the narrator gradually prepare the reader for the revelation of what happened in September? Refer to lines 1–28. — 10
6. Analyse the narrative technique. How does it determine the way the reader sees both Shukumar and his wife? — 20

## II. Composition

Choose *one* of the following topics. Write about 250 to 300 words. — 50

1. Treasure your relationships, not your possessions.
2. Family affairs. Choose a work of literature by an English-speaking author and show how this topic is treated.

3. Write up Shoba's entry in her diary six months after the death of her baby. What are her secret thoughts and wishes concerning her relationship with Shukumar?
4. Is this correlation inevitable?

From: www.cartoonstock.com

## III. Translation

*The text is an excerpt from an interview with Jhumpa Lahiri after she had been rewarded the Pulitzer Prize.*

Translate the following text into German: 50/200

When I was growing up in Rhode Island in the 1970s I felt neither Indian nor American. Like many immigrant offspring I felt intense pressure to be two things, loyal to the old world and fluent in the new. Looking back, I see this was generally the case. But my perception as a young girl was that I fell short at both ends, shuffling between two dimensions that had nothing to do with one another.

When I first started writing I was not conscious that my subject was the Indian-American experience. What drew me to my craft was the desire to force the two worlds I occupied to mingle on the page as I was not brave enough, or mature enough, to allow in life. My first book was published in 1999, and since then the term "Indian-American"[1] has become part of this country's vocabulary. I've heard it so often that these days, if asked about my background, I use the term myself, pleasantly surprised that I do not have to explain further. What a difference from my early life, when there was no such way to describe me, when the most I could do was to clumsily and ineffectually explain.

From: Newsweek, March 6, 2006

Anmerkungen
1 "Indian-American": not to be translated here

## Lösungsvorschlag

### I. Questions on the text

1. *You will find evidence for your answer in paragraphs 2 and 4. Mind the double question.*

   In September, while Shoba was expecting their baby, Shukumar had attended an academic conference. His wife had persuaded him to go as the contacts there might come in useful for his career plans. During the convention Shukumar received a phone message from the hospital which informed him about Shoba's critical state. When he arrived the baby had been stillborn, after an emergency caesarean. There is no indication in the text that Shukumar can be blamed for the misfortune. His wife had explicitly urged him to go, and the due date of the birth was still three weeks away. All the necessary precautions had been taken, phone and flight numbers were noted, and a friend would take Shoba to the hospital in case of complications.

2. *Here you need not separate ideas from feelings. Make sure to analyse the facts. The information is to be found in the third paragraph.*

   The size of the cab overwhelms Shukumar. He feels "dwarfed" (l. 17) in it and compares it with their own small car. This may have given him the idea to welcome an enlargement of his family, to have children of his own. He fantasizes about getting a big station wagon, driving the kids to their various appointments, rather conventionally with himself at the wheel and his wife looking after the children on the back seat. For the first time in his married life he casts away his doubts about being a parent without having the security of a job and "welcome[s] the image" (l. 23) of a happy family.

3. *This question only refers to their attitude towards <u>work</u>.*

   Before the events of September Shukumar had been a "mediocre" (l. 41) student at graduate school who dutifully complied with his academic assignments and a teaching obligation, without much enthusiasm and in keeping with his "elusive" nature (ll. 40/41). His slack attitude to work is illustrated by the fact that "he was still a student at thirty-five" (l. 22). Afterwards, he hardly makes any effort any more – he can't even summon up enough energy to leave his bed in the morning or the house on small errands. Even when he is temporarily relieved from his teaching classes to be able to concentrate on his dissertation, his work does not progress. In short: "… nothing was pushing Shukumar" (l. 51). His wife, on the other hand, appears to have been a dedicated worker even before the events. She has her own office where she meticulously proofreads manuscripts. Her responsible attitude towards work also becomes clear when she makes her husband attend the conference to further his career. After the baby's death she deliberately increases her work load. She leaves the house early, before her husband has woken up, works overtime at her office, even brings documents home to work on them at the weekends and starts new projects.

4. Their relationship has suffered a strong setback. Before the loss of the baby they had cared for each other and were interested in each other's work. Now they avoid each other and never communicate about their grief. Shoba buries herself in work, leaves the house before Shukumar is about and seems to stay out as much as she can. He lets himself go and has become negligent with his domestic duties. When both are in they are hardly to be found in the same room and try to spend as little time together as possible, even at the weekends. They still have occasional sex but without their former tenderness (ll. 55 ff).

5. In the first paragraph the reader wonders about the state of the couple's relationship and Shukumar's unexplained negligence with himself. Something must have happened six months ago (l. 6). The author then brings up Shoba's pregnancy, her husband's departure and the emergency measures, which is ominous, especially when their leave-taking is described as the "last moment he saw Shoba pregnant" (l. 14). An experienced reader will perceive Shukumar's subsequent anticipation of a happy family life as ironic, which is confirmed when the hospital tries to reach him at the conference.

6. *For narrative technique see 'Tips for questions on the text – Analyse the perspective/point of view'.*

   The text is written from the perspective of a third-person narrator with a limited point of view. The reader sees everything through Shukumar's eyes – he thought (l. 14), he imagined (l. 18), he felt (l. 17), he knew (l. 27), he had believed (l. 58). His behaviour, his opinions and reflections, the occurrences as well as what he relates about his wife, all this is filtered through what he decides to communicate. Thus the reader cannot be sure what Shoba feels and how she really copes with the loss of her child. One can only guess her constitution from the text which mentions that she delves herself into work.

## II. Composition

1. Modern society is all about consuming, possessing and showing off how much money one has spent – which only serves one's superficial material needs or desires. No deeper benefit can be gained. People will only be satisfied for a limited period of time before the next thing catches their attention and is desperately craved for, only to be replaced by yet another vanity.
   Relationships, however, can give infinitely more to human beings. Be it friendship, love or family – contact with others is indispensable. Relationships are much more consistent and rewarding than objects. They can give a person strength and support in times of need and double your joy when you can share it. What is the use of a luxury car or a villa at the seaside if you have no real friends or family you can enjoy them with? Relationships are about giving and taking, loving and being loved, and you get so much back from the people you care about. Somebody without social and personal relations can never be really happy when he derives his satisfaction from his belongings alone. Something essential will be missing to make his life more worth living.
   Consuming is easy, it doesn't take much to buy something. Building up a relationship, however, takes time, courage, honesty and willpower. It does not come flying into your arms, you have to work on it. In the process you learn a lot about yourself and about the reactions of others to you. All in all, I think our relationship with other people is one of the most valuable gifts a person can receive and cannot be replaced by worldly possessions.

   *(This essay was written by Vanessa Spiller, a student at Max-Planck-Gymnasium, Munich, and was only slightly altered.)*

2. *'Family affairs' is a fairly vague term. You may interpret it as you please. A 'work of literature' is anything from a play, a novel, a short story or a poem from your school's syllabus or your own private reading you are familiar with. As for plays,* Romeo and Juliet *contains interesting aspects about two hostile families reconciled after the triumph and tragedy of love. Lorraine Hansberry's* A Raisin in the Sun *would also qualify. In the following novels you can also find sufficient references to family affairs: Susan Townsend's* Diary of Adrian Mole, Dead Poets Society *by Nancy Kleinbaum*

*(though it is only adapted from a film), J. D. Salinger's* Catcher in the Rye*, or the Utopian novels* Brave New World *by Aldous Huxley (where the concept of family is abolished), and Lois Lowry's* The Giver.
*Begin by giving a brief summary, describe the family situation and show how the subject is treated (interpretation, narrative technique). Our example is about the* Catcher in the Rye.

*The Catcher in the Rye* is a novel of initiation. It is the story of Holden Caulfield, an adolescent who tries to come to grips with the world as he sees it. Expelled from yet another prep school he decides to spend a few days on his own before facing his parents. He lives through various encounters with the 'real' world, including friends from his past and his little sister Phoebe, and ends up confused and desperate in a mental institution. His central concern is the 'phoniness' of people. Though he interacts with many individuals none of them have as much impact on him as certain members of his family. His parents are hardly mentioned, only his mother is given a short and unimpressive appearance. His father is a lawyer who plays the game of the 'phonies'. His elder brother D. B. is no role model for him either – he makes money as a scriptwriter for the film industry, which he detests for their triviality. The only people he truly admires are his brother Allie, who died early, and his little sister Phoebe. To him Allie, who never had the chance to grow up, and Phoebe, personify the innocence of children who are untouched by conventions and insincerity. In the end it is Phoebe who makes him understand the impossibility of persisting in his immature fantasies and his arrogance in judging other people. The author presents Holden as teller and protagonist of his own story, which induces the reader to sympathise with him and share his views. The novel proceeds in a chronological order, interrupted by frequent flashbacks, within a frame that presents Holden at the clinic, beginning and ending his story there. Irony is abundant and reflects Holden's criticism of people and the way of the world, but is never used with the two siblings he adores. The ending points towards the possibility that Holden may finally have started to come to terms with reality.

3. *Diary writing is a private affair. You do it for yourself, to discover what you think and feel, to express thoughts you don't want to share with others, to be able to remember what happened. It also permits you to honestly reflect problems and your behaviour. Often it helps you to cope with disagreeable situations. When you write an entry to Shoba's diary you can fill the gap the narrator has left by not supplying her thoughts and feelings.*

Dear diary,

I don't really know what to do! My life has suffered such a fundamental change since I had my stillborn baby. Nobody can understand the shock and despair that came over me when I woke up from the delivery. Shukumar tried to be sweet about it but somehow I feel he did not fully comprehend what this tragedy meant to me. We haven't been able to talk too much since I left the hospital – it is clear that he avoids me but I don't know why. Does he blame me, maybe for making him attend the conference? He couldn't have saved the baby anyway. I never had the impression that he was so keen on having children! So what is eating him? He has stopped working and helping me in the house altogether, hardly goes out anymore and pretends to sleep until I leave for work. Our married life has become a disaster, we don't seem to be able to share anything anymore. Well, we do make love sometimes but not the way we used to, there is no tenderness in it, no warmth, no affection.
I really would like to make a new beginning with him, I know he needs me and I still love him, but this love is wearing thinner every day. Yet the idea of talking it all over with him before all is lost scares me. What if it makes things even worse? I think I will

write him a letter first and implore him to come to me, to take me in his arms and be my husband again.

4. *Be careful – this is not the usual 'Comment on the cartoon' task! The topical question asks you to discuss the correlation between career and the functioning of marriages. The best way to tackle this is to use the illustration in your introduction and then proceed to write an argumentative composition.*

   The cartoon shows either an economic analyst or, more ironically, a dishevelled businessman working in front of a chart depicting a mirror image of the correlation between professional performance and its effects on people's marriages. Is this some kind of a joke or is there some truth in this message?
   The key words are energy and time, the energy and time you invest in your work and in your relationship with your spouse. It seems to be a truism that excelling professionally leads to neglecting your commitment to your partner at home. What comes to one's mind is the image of a workaholic who can hardly tear himself away from his office, brings his work home and is so absorbed in it that he can barely think of little else. Even in their sleep these people are pursued by problems and solutions. At the breakfast table they study the business section of the paper and can hardly wait to rush back to the company. This scenario is unfailingly bound for the destruction of your marriage, as there remains little room for interest in your partner's needs, in building your lives and spending time together. It implies a collision course to frustration, estrangement and the break-up of your marriage.
   People, however, by nature will have jobs they intend to do well, and will have a certain degree of ambition. It is difficult to imagine that most of them are heading for a divorce. There must be a way of reconciling career goals and married life. The secret of being successful in both areas probably lies in noticing the danger signs in time: criticism, dissatisfaction, disappointment about your withdrawal from shared activities, your own guilty conscience. Most couples seem to be wise enough to react and mend their ways instead of driving their marriage against the wall. Nobody can seriously wish to place professional progress above a happy marriage. After all, your family, more than anything else, serves as a valuable base of support to help you succeed in your work.

## III. Translation

In meiner Kindheit[1] in den 1970er-Jahren in Rhode Island, fühlte ich mich weder als Inderin noch als Amerikanerin. Wie viele Nachkommen von Einwanderern bedrückte es mich immens, gleichzeitig[2] zwei Dinge bewältigen zu müssen – loyal gegenüber der alten Welt zu sein und mich reibungslos[3] in der neuen zurechtzufinden. Wenn ich zurückblicke, sehe ich, dass dies auch im Großen und Ganzen der Fall war. Meine eigene[1] Wahrnehmung als junges Mädchen war jedoch, dass ich beiden Zielen nicht gerecht wurde und zwischen zwei Welten[4], die nichts miteinander zu tun hatten, hin und her pendelte.

Als ich zu schreiben begann[5], war es mir nicht bewusst, dass mein Thema die indisch-amerikanische Erfahrung war. Was mich zu meinem Handwerk hinzog, war das Verlangen, die beiden Welten, die ich bewohnte, dazu zu zwingen, sich auf dem Papier[6] zu vereinen, da ich weder den Mut noch die Reife dafür besaß, dies im richtigen[2] Leben zuzulassen. Mein erstes Buch wurde 1999 veröffentlicht, und inzwischen[7] ist der Begriff „Indian-American" in den Sprachgebrauch dieses Landes eingegangen. Ich habe ihn schon[2] so oft gehört, dass ich, wenn man mich heute nach meiner Herkunft fragt, diesen Ausdruck selbst verwende und dabei[2] angenehm überrascht bin, dass ich dazu[2] nichts weiter erklären muss. Welch ein Unterschied zu meinen jüngeren Jahren[8], als es keine solche Möglichkeit gab, mich zu beschreiben, als das Beste[9], was ich tun konnte, war, umständliche und untaugliche[10] Erklärungen zu geben.

Anmerkungen

1 Natürlich geht auch: *Als ich ... aufwuchs*

2 Stilistisch bedingte Einfügungen

3 *Fluent* (fließend, flüssig) bezieht sich eher nicht auf die Sprachkenntnisse; ‚*reibungslos ... zurechtfinden*' drückt am ehesten aus, was gemeint ist.

4 *Dimensionen* ist natürlich auch möglich, gefällt uns aber nicht so gut, auch wenn man *Welten* wiederholen muss.

5 *First* darf hier nicht übersetzt zu werden, weil der Ausdruck im Deutschen dann einen anderen Sinn bekäme (Zuerst – und dann?).

6 *Seite,* vor allem im Singular, passt hier nicht. *Papier* kommt am Nächsten.

7 *Seitdem* hätte einen zu engen Bezug zum Erscheinen des Buchs – als ob es damit etwas zu tun gehabt hätte.

8 *Meinem früheren Leben* klingt zu esoterisch (Seelenwanderung?); möglich wäre auch: *Als ich zum ersten Mal zur Feder griff ...*

9 Besseres Deutsch als *das Meiste. Höchstens* wäre auch eine Möglichkeit.

10 *Ineffectual* heißt wörtlich *wirkungslos,* auch *halbherzig* findet sich im Wörterbuch, trifft aber die Sachlage nicht so gut.

## Leistungskurs Englisch 2009
## Textaufgabe I

**How to save a billion lives**
**A war against the weed spreads and escalates**

Even more than tempting liquors like tequila, tobacco is a pleasure that the Old World wishes it had never taken from the New. In 1492, when Christopher Columbus was met by tribesmen with "fruit, wooden spears and certain dried leaves which gave off a distinct fragrance", he threw the last gift away. But his shipmates brought home the custom of sucking in the smoke, and the taste spread so rapidly that in 1604 King James I of England was prompted to issue a denunciation of the "manifold abuses of this vile custome[1]".

Vile indeed, but habit-forming and therefore lethally dangerous: it cuts short the lives of between a third and a half of its practitioners. According to the World Health Organization (WHO), perhaps 100 m people died prematurely during the 20th century as a result of tobacco, making it the leading preventable cause of death and one of the top killers overall. Another 1 billion more may die from it in this century if current trends continue unchecked.

In recent years smoking has been sharply restricted in some unlikely places. In 2004 Ireland amazed the world by successfully imposing a tobacco ban on all workplaces; and at the start of this year France's café culture suddenly went smoke-free. The draconian curbs introduced by California in 1998 have been followed, at least in part, by well over half America's states. But the number of smokers in China, India and other developing countries is continuing to grow, as addiction spreads faster than information.

Hence the determination of almost everybody involved in global public health to escalate the war on smoking. Over 150 countries have already ratified the Framework Convention on Tobacco Control, which requires countries to take a range of anti-smoking measures. Last July negotiators agreed on international norms for banning smoking in public places.

In addition to new international rules, the WHO is pushing for aggressive policies at national and local levels. On February 7th Margaret Chan, the WHO's director-general and Michael Bloomberg, New York's zealously anti-smoking mayor, were due to unveil the most comprehensive survey of tobacco use ever carried out. The venue was fitting. Tom Frieden, the city's health commissioner, notes that the mayor's efforts have reduced smoking among the adults in New York by 20 % and among teenagers in public schools by 50 %. Mr Bloomberg's private charity, which supports many anti-smoking efforts worldwide also funded the global survey, known as MPOWER.

The study is "a call to action to avoid a public-health catastrophe", says Douglas Bettcher, head of the Tobacco Free Initiative at the WHO. The report lists the anti-smoking efforts of countries worldwide, offering benchmarks for aspiring reformers. What the survey shows, says Dr Bettcher, is that most countries have yet to implement even those policies that are proven to work.

The WHO says countries must do six related things. The first is to improve the quality of data on tobacco use. The second is to impose sweeping Irish-style smoking bans; only 5 % of the global population is now covered by such curbs. The third is to intensify efforts to induce and assist smokers to drop the habit. Only nine countries offer the kind of well-funded, accessible programmes of which the WHO approves.

Those ideas concern the existing users of tobacco; another three are aimed at persuading people not to light up in the first place. It may be hard to believe, but WHO insists that most smokers still do not understand the full extent of the health risks. It wants all countries to mandate large, grotesque pictorial warnings on cigarette packets. Another policy proven to work (in the handful of countries, representing 5 % of the world's population, to have tried it) is a complete ban on marketing. The agency is adamant that "partial bans on tobacco advertising, promotion and sponsorship do not work."

The final prescription offered by the WHO is also the most powerful one: higher taxes. Studies show that raising tobacco taxes by a tenth may cause a 4 % drop in consumption in rich countries and an 8 % drop in poor ones, with tax revenue rising despite lower sales. The agency wants a 70 % increase in the retail price of tobacco, which it says could prevent up to a quarter of tobacco-related deaths worldwide. The claim is that higher taxes not only bring in revenue to fund anti-smoking efforts; they actually benefit the poor.

How come? A forthcoming paper by two scholars (Jonathan Gruber of the Massachusetts Institute of Technology and Botond Koszegi of the University of California) notes that smokers face a familiar choice between short-term pleasure and a long-term desire to quit. Tobacco taxes are an incentive to make the right choice, and because the poor are price-sensitive, they benefit the most.

The practical argument for action is simpler: the tobacco industry is getting the world's poor hooked before governments can respond. In recent years, as rich countries have clamped down on smoking, tobacco firms have shifted their focus to poorer places. A study by Britain's Bath University found that by using aggressive tactics, such as targeting women, international tobacco firms had helped to double smoking rates in Russia in 1991.

The tobacco industry is regrouping in order to focus on "promising" markets and escape the pesky lawsuits it is likely to face in rich, litigious countries. For example, Altria[2] plans to spin off Philip Morris International as a stand-alone foreign entity in late March. China is now home to more than a quarter of the world's smokers; it will soon be manufacturing Marlboro cigarettes for Philip Morris, and the firm will be exporting Chinese tobacco to other countries.

At times, the strategy used by public-health campaigners may seem heavy-handed; they retort that nothing else can work against a rich adversary. Indeed, Dr Bettcher argues that just as mosquitoes convey Malaria, Big Tobacco is the "vector spreading this epidemic". And eradicating tobacco may prove every bit as hard as fighting insect-borne disease.

From: *The Economist,* February 7, 2008

1 custome: outdated spelling of the word 'custom'

2 Altria: global tobacco concern based in the USA

**Worksheet: How to save a billion lives**

maximum number
of points attainable

## I. Questions on the text

Read all the questions first, then answer them in the given order. Use your own words as far as is appropriate.

1. Sum up the measures that have already been taken to counteract the negative effects of smoking and explain why they are necessary. 20
2. According to the article, what remains to be done in the fight against smoking? 15
3. Describe the efforts that have been made by the tobacco industry to minimize their financial losses. 10
4. Comment on the function of the headline and subtitle as well as the last paragraph of the text. What do they reveal about the author's personal attitude to the topic? 20
5. What purpose does the first paragraph serve? Outline in detail the writer's intentions. 15
6. Analyse the use of language. What does it tell us about the reader the text is intended for? 20

## II. Composition

Choose *one* of the following topics. Write about 250 to 300 words. 50

1. Surfing the Internet – a dangerous addiction or a wonderful feature of modern life?
2. "Alcohol advertising places profit before health and should be forbidden by law."
   Write a speech for or against this statement that you will deliver in a debating society.
3. Written warnings on cigarette packets are not enough and should be accompanied by shocking pictures (cf. ll. 44/45). Discuss.
4. Analyse the cartoon and comment on its message.

http://www.politicalcartoons.com

## III. Translation

Translate the following text into German: 50/200

### A Drug to End Drug Addiction

What if science made a pill to protect us from addiction – keeping us from smoking cigarettes, getting fat or abusing drugs and alcohol? According to encouraging results from several lines of study, it seems that day may be closer than we thought. Researchers in labs around the world are now developing vaccines to inoculate people against dangerously addictive substances such as cocaine and heroin.

Unlike traditional anti-addiction approaches, such as psychotherapy and older medications like methadone for heroin addicts, vaccines prevent the addictive substance from ever reaching the user's brain – that is, they inhibit the addictive cycle rather than respond to it. The goal is to eliminate the chemical cascade that results in the euphoric 'high', which, in turn, sparks addiction – what a comedian once described this way. "What does cocaine make you feel like? It makes you feel like having more cocaine."

As complicated as the puzzle of addiction may be, Koslen[1] believes that the 21st century war against drug abuse can be waged as successfully as last century's global fight against infectious disease. It may not be a magic pill, but Koslen hopes the vaccine will be the first step along the road to recovery for many addicts.

From: *Time,* January 9, 2008

Annotation
1 Koslen: the psychiatry professor whose team is developing the vaccine

---

## Lösungsvorschlag

## I. Questions on the text

1. *You will easily find these measures in ll. 14–23 and could also mention Mr Bloomberg's efforts (ll. 28ff). You could mention, as a key word, the prevention of a public-health catastrophe in line 32.*

   In 2004 Ireland prohibited smoking in all workplaces, and France banned tobacco in coffeehouses at the beginning of 2008 to protect non-smokers. As early as 1998 California introduced severe regulations to restrain smoking which were partly taken over by more than half of the American states. A Framework Convention on Tobacco Control to implement a number of anti-smoking measures has been signed by more than 150 countries, and in 2007 norms for banning smoking in public places were accepted internationally (l. 23). In New York smoking among adults and teenagers has gone down significantly, due to the mayor's efforts (ll. 28 ff.).
   The fight against tobacco is necessary as it considerably shortens the life expectancy of its users. Around 100 m people died as a consequence of smoking in the 20th century, and another billion are expected to die from it if nothing is done (l. 12 f.). Smoking is one of the 'top killers' (l. 11) and may lead to a 'public health catastrophe' (l. 32).

2. *The answer to this question is fairly easy. All the information ('six related things') is given between lines 37 and 55. By the way, the 15 credits allotted here are based on the 5 for content and 5 for language scheme, multiplied by 1.5.*

   The WHO has made six suggestions to intensify the war on tobacco. First, the database on smoking has to be improved. Second, the Irish example has to be enforced worldwide – so far only 5 percent of the world's countries have taken this step. Third, more programmes must be offered to smokers to help them drop their habit. Another set of measures should be directed towards people who might be tempted to start smoking. This could be done by printing large explicit pictures on the cigarette packets to illustrate the health risks of smoking. It would also help to prohibit advertisements and commercials altogether. According to the WHO the most efficient measure would be to raise taxes on tobacco, the higher the better.

3. *The tobacco industry's reactions can be found from lines 61 to 72. The task expects you to 'describe' their efforts, a term which seems exaggerated in a 10-credit question. The few lines that refer to the question don't give much ground for description. It is ok when you just answer the question in your own words.*

   To make up for their financial losses due to anti-smoking campaigns the tobacco industry is trying to raise the smoking rate among the world's poor before their governments also start taking measures. Another strategy is to target specific sections of the population, as they did with women in Russia, doubling the sales of cigarettes there. They are also shifting their marketing efforts to new and 'promising' (l. 67) markets like China, where they don't run the risk of losing costly lawsuits filed by victims of smoking. The global Altria concern plans to establish a new headquarter in this country, where already more than a fourth of the world's smokers live, and to export Chinese tobacco from there to other countries (ll. 70–72).

4. *Mind that you will have to consider 4 points here: the functions of the headline, the subtitle and the last paragraph and what these indicate about the author's attitude. It is advisable to divide your answer into 4 sections to make sure you don't forget any of the questions.*

   Apart from hinting at the content of the article the headline catches the reader's attention by offering a kind of manual for a stupendous task – how to save a billion lives, without suggesting a solution right away, which makes it even more interesting.
   The subtitle is similarly enigmatic: What kind of war is going on and even escalating? What weed might this be? In the last paragraph the author returns to the tobacco weed and the subject of war. He compares the Tobacco Industry to a malaria-carrying mosquito – both are spreading a disastrous epidemic – and justifies the intensity of the anti-smoking campaign with the argument that both 'diseases' are equally dangerous and hard to eradicate.
   The author is clearly against smoking. From the outset he mentions that billions of lives are at stake unless an all-out war is waged against tobacco, whose effects are as deadly as is malaria. The title suggests that he thinks this war can be won.

5. *Here we have a double question – the purpose of the first paragraph and the author's intention in beginning his article in this way.*

   In his introduction the author seems to entertain the reader with quaint references to the historical origins of the smoking habit in Europe, with the different reactions of Columbus, his crew and King James I. It is quite surprising and curious that the sombre tone of the title and headline is not continued here.
   Yet, by immediately branding the pleasure of smoking as a habit "the Old World wishes it had never taken from the New" (l. 1 f.) he leaves no doubt as to his own opinion. Both Columbus, who "threw the last gift away" (l. 4), and King James, who recognized the vileness of the habit as early as 1604, are used as his witnesses for the denunciation of tobacco.

6. *We suggest beginning with the second part of the question, as the answer is quite obvious, and then proceeding to the evidence based on the author's language use.*

The text appeared in the Economist, which is a quality magazine for educated readers who enjoy elaborate language and precise analyses, and are familiar with economic and world affairs.
Consequently, the author's language is factual – he introduces figures (e. g. in line 10), statistics (ll. 51 f.), surveys (l. 27) and research results (ll. 56 ff.). At the same time he uses hard words like draconian (l. 16), to mandate (l. 45), vector (l. 75), or economic and political terms like ratified (l. 21) or benchmarks (l. 34) which only an educated reader would be familiar with. To make his article stylistically more elegant he also works with devices like antithesis (Old World – New [World], ll. 1 f.; short term pleasure – long-term desire, l. 58), personification (a war against the weed, subtitle), comparison (mosquitoes and the Tobacco Industry, l. 75) and alliteration (tempting … like tequila, tobacco, l. 1, covered by … curbs, l. 39). His readers will also be amused by his inclusion of outdated expressions in the historical passages (sucking in the smoke, l. 5; manifold, l. 6; vile custome, ll. 6/7).

## II. Composition

1. *This topic requires an argumentative approach, with introduction, discussion of the pros and cons, and your personal conclusion. Before you start it is advisable to assemble some key words for each position:*

| *Dangers* | *Advantages* |
|---|---|
| *risk of social isolation* | *research* |
| *playing and gaming* | *forums* |
| *trusting all information* | *shopping and banking* |
| *children* | *contacts* |
| *illegal downloads* | *email* |
| *virus infections* | *legal downloads and services* |
| *phishing* | *games* |

*Due to the limited number of words you cannot discuss all points – so select the ones you think important or which you know most about. Don't forget to include examples.*

The other day I bought a new mobile phone on the Internet after I had studied some test results and found the cheapest seller. Of course I had to give my credit card details, which made me a little uneasy. There is always the question of whether the dangers of going online outweigh the advantages.
Isn't the Internet a wonderful feature of modern life? How often have I consulted Wikipedia to do some research for my homework! What would I do to stay in contact with my friends if I was deprived of email? On sites like Facebook I can chat with people all over the world! There is always a forum I can consult for all kinds of problems, and where I can study the suggestions of experts. Running a computer often requires software updates which can be downloaded in no time, as well as new programmes or games. I can even watch television on my PC or Champions League games, which are not broadcast on regular channels.
At the same time I am well aware of the dangers which lurk behind all these benefits. Viruses or spyware can cause serious damage to your PC or infiltrate your data. If you are not careful enough, phishing can lead to severe financial losses. By downloading music illegally you come into conflict with the law. As helpful as research on the Internet may be – if you use it uncritically your results will not be worth much.
What can really get you addicted are online games or Second Life, where you can get so absorbed that you lose your sense of time, where you even forget to eat or drink and have no interest in anything else. As a consequence you may neglect your responsibili-

ties, your grades at school will suffer, your family will get furious with you and you risk losing your friends. Many people are so addicted to their computers that they neglect their social relationships.
All things considered, I am a hundred percent in favour of the Internet and wouldn't want to miss it. The main point is to treat it with discretion, to be critical of its contents, and to monitor yourself enough not to get addicted. The Internet is a wonderful feature of modern life, but it is up to us to use it wisely.

2. *In a formal debate the first speaker usually defends a proposition by giving his arguments as convincingly as possible, within a limited time span. His aim is to obtain a majority for his case among the audience at the end of the debate. Formally his speech is structured in an opening statement, a main body with his arguments, and a conclusion. Remember to use some expressions which refer to an audience.*

Madam Chairman and distinguished members of this society,

It is my firm conviction that alcohol advertising places profit before health and should be forbidden by law without exceptions, in any medium and in any form.
Let me begin by directing your attention to the ultimate purpose of advertising, namely the promotion of goods to increase their sales, and thereby increase the producers' profits. So far so good, but what if the products are alcoholic beverages, which nobody needs and whose consumption causes serious problems rather than improving the quality of our lives?
It is a well-known fact that alcohol every year contributes to millions of deaths worldwide, which can easily be confirmed by consulting medical statistics. Excessive drinking leads to cirrhosis or cancer of the liver in the long run. Recent research has shown that it eventually may also lead to irreversible brain damage. Apart from these depressing prognoses any consumption of alcohol affects virtually all senses and organs of the body, as it goes directly into the bloodstream. Regular drinkers run a significantly higher risk of contracting a heart disease later in their lives. As side effects, alcohol will alter your perception and slow down your reaction time – not the best conditions for driving a vehicle and surviving on the road! Just like smoking, drinking is addictive. It may lead to alcoholism, a condition that will not only ruin your health but also isolate you from your social contacts.
Ladies and gentlemen, I am more than sure that I have proved the point that alcohol ruins people's health. Why then should anybody get away with promoting the destruction of our health to make profits? Why do we still allow the producers of alcohol to seduce our children to binge drinking, to create the illusion that drinking makes us happier or more successful? Let us close the curtain on alcohol advertising once and for all; let us make it as illegal as selling drugs. I rest my case, thank you for your attention.

3. *The reference in the topic gives you a good hint at how to introduce your composition.*

To smoke or not to smoke – is this the question? The World Health Organization and over 150 countries think it isn't. They are determined to reduce smoking drastically and have already seen to it that written warnings are displayed on cigarette packets. Now the WHO insists that "large, grotesque pictorial warnings" should accompany them. Would this really further reduce smoking?
When written warnings first appeared, buyers of cigarettes probably looked with a certain, if not amused interest at notices like 'Smoking kills' or 'Smoking clogs the arteries'. It is unlikely that they dropped their ciggies into the nearest waste bin in terror. Don't we all have to die sooner or later? My arteries are just fine, thank you very

much! Such may have been the first reactions, to be followed by a shrug of the shoulders and an attitude of 'Carry on, smoker, enjoy the good time'.
The proponents of stark pictorial warnings are convinced that this tactic would reduce smoking far more effectively. People who are indifferent to written warnings might be shocked to see pictures of a dead body in the morgue, of a lung destroyed by a tumour, or of a surgery on an open heart, in colour and full detail. After all, a picture speaks a thousand words, as the proverb says. In order to deter people from smoking you need more than words like 'Smoking can cause a slow and painful death'; you have to emphasize the harsh consequences; you need to show them a real person with his face eaten up by mouth cancer, at least in a photograph!
The first surveys from countries that have already adopted pictorial warnings show that they do work. They may not accomplish a substantial decline in smoking, however. This could only be achieved by making it illegal, which would be disproportionate and interfere with the free will of people who have the right to delude themselves.

4. *It says in the task that you should analyse the cartoon, which can only mean that a lengthy description at the cost of comment would not be welcome. The message is obviously expressed in the headings of the two parts.*

The cartoon consists of two related parts that play on Apple's "iProducts". The frame contains images of their well-known gadgets like the iMac or the iPhone and states that these devices allow people to interact, network and socialize. The actual cartoon presents a man in front of a café who has to do his smoking outside and is denoted as an "iSmoke". The fact that this person is obliged to indulge his vice in unfavourable circumstances – he looks unhappy, partly because of the cold and the blowing wind, and partly because he is deprived of company – brings us to the message of the cartoonist: Even if modern electronic devices are often criticized as unsociable, they aren't when compared to the vice of smoking.
Let us face the facts and begin with the devices. While an iMac is a computer, which can indeed be used to socialize with other people on forums or through email, and an iPhone is the latest cell phone, whose communicative potential is beyond doubt, the same can hardly be said about the other three. An iPod is a portable media player, which can store a multitude of video and audio-files and is mainly used to play music, preferably acquired from Apple's iTune download store. From a social point-of-view, who would approach a person with his ears plugged to a device and intent on removing himself from this world to a constant stream of music?
The image of the smoker in the cartoon, on the other hand, is not quite fair. He may stand in the cold wind all by himself, but is this reality? It is true that non-smokers will turn away from him when he lights a cigarette, but rumour has it that you often find groups of smokers outside restaurants and on balconies who enjoy themselves tremendously, animatedly talking to people they would never have contacted otherwise. After all, they are a special and even persecuted group who have to stick together.
The message of the cartoon is inaccurate and not quite serious and principally ows its effect to the temptation of having a good joke with the puns on devices/vices and iApple/ iSmoke – which is rather funny.

## III. Translation

Eine Droge, die mit der Drogenabhängigkeit Schluss macht

Was wäre, wenn die Wissenschaft eine Pille herstellen würde, die uns vor dem Abhängigwerden bewahrt – die uns davon abhält, Zigaretten zu rauchen, dick zu werden oder Drogen und Alkohol zu missbrauchen? Als Folge vielversprechender Ergebnisse aus mehreren Studienreihen[1] scheint[2] dieser Tag näher zu sein als wir bisher[7] annahmen. Forscher in Labors auf der ganzen Welt sind dabei Impfstoffe zu entwickeln, um Menschen gegen hochgradig süchtig machende[3] Stoffe wie Kokain und Heroin zu immunisieren[4].

Anders als herkömmliche Ansätze[5] zur Suchtbekämpfung, wie etwa die Psychotherapie und ältere medikamentöse Behandlungen[6] wie Methadon für Heroinabhängige, verhindern Impfstoffe, dass die süchtig machende Substanz überhaupt das Gehirn des Drogenkonsumenten erreicht – das heißt, dass diese Impfstoffe[7] den Suchtkreislauf hemmen, anstatt[8] auf ihn einzuwirken[9]. Das Ziel ist es, die chemische Kettenreaktion[10] auszuschalten, die zu dem Hochgefühl[11] führt, welches wiederum die Abhängigkeit auslöst. Ein Komiker hat das einmal so ausgedrückt: „Worauf macht dir Kokain Lust? Auf noch mehr Kokain."

So vertrackt[12] das Puzzle[13] der Abhängigkeit auch sein mag, so glaubt Koslen dennoch[7], dass der Krieg gegen Drogenmissbrauch im 21. Jahrhundert genauso erfolgreich geführt werden kann wie der weltweite Kampf gegen ansteckende Krankheiten im letzten Jahrhundert. Es mag sich dabei[7] nicht um eine Wunderpille[14] handeln, aber Koslen hofft, dass der Impfstoff für viele Süchtige der erste Schritt in Richtung Heilung sein wird.

Anmerkungen

1 *Forschungszweigen* wäre auch möglich
2 Auch: *mag es den Anschein haben, dass ...*
3 Oder: *Stoffe mit hohem Suchtpotential*
4 *inoculate* heißt zwar wörtlich *impfen*, wäre aber eine teilweise Wiederholung von *Impfstoffe*
5 wörtlich: *Annäherungen, Vorgehensweisen*
6 Möglich wäre auch nur *Medikamente*
7 stilistisch bedingte Einfügungen
8 *Eher ... als* ist falsch: der Kreislauf wird komplett verhindert!
9 Näher an der Grundbedeutung wäre: *auf ihn zu reagieren*
10 Der Ausdruck ist in diesem Zusammenhang schwerlich gut zu übersetzen. Eigentlich ist es ein kleinerer oder Teil eines Wasserfalls, auch eine schnelle Abfolge von Geschehnissen. Akzeptiert würden wahrscheinlich auch: *Stufenleiter, Kaskade, Schwall*
11 Notfalls auch: *euphorisches Hoch* oder ‚*High*'
12 *kompliziert* ist auch in Ordnung
13 Auch: *Rätsel*
14 Auch: *Wunderdroge, Zauberpille*

## Small Island

by Andrea Levy

*It is the year 1948. Hortense Roberts, who is the narrator, and Gilbert Joseph, who fought for England in World War II, live in Jamaica.*

'Married!' Mrs Anderson[1] yelled. 'But how long have you known each other?'

'Oh, now, let me see … Five days.' Gilbert said.

'It will be three weeks and five days by the time we are married,' I explained.

'And three weeks and six days will have passed when I sail to England to see the place is nice for the arrival of my new wife,' Gilbert added.

There was complete silence at the table – even the old woman ceased sucking her chicken bone to stare on us. Suddenly Mrs Anderson pushed back her hair, leaped from her seat and wrapped her arms round me before moving on to Gilbert, whom she hugged so tight his head almost disappeared into the crease of her bust.

'So you like jazz, Gilbert?' was all Mrs Anderson wanted to know.

Returning to England was more than an ambition for Gilbert Joseph. It was a mission, a calling, even a duty. This man was so restless he could not stay still. Always in motion he was agitated, impatient – like a petulant boy waiting his turn at cricket. He told me opportunity opened in England as abundant as fruit on Jamaican trees. And he was going to be the man to pluck it.

'Your brother still there?' he asked.

'My brother?'

'This Michael you ask me of – your brother – he still in England?'

'Perhaps he is,' I told him.

'Well, you must let me know his address and I can look him up for you.'

But this big-ideas man had no money. He had spent all his money, he confided to me, on bees.

'On bees?' I asked.

He had some crazy notion about honey producing money. His cousin in St Mary convinced him that keeping bees was foolproof. All he had to do was give his cousin the money to buy hives, jars and printed labels and soon the money from the honey would send Gilbert winging to England.

'But,' he told me, 'this cousin of mine lost the bees,'

'How you lose bees?' I asked.

His reply? 'It is not easy, but it can be done.'

This small setback had left him undeterred. He had another money-making idea. Postcards. Tourists, he told me, who were now flocking to this island for sun and rum need postcards – pictures, scenes of the many wonders of Jamaica to send back to their family at home. He would swiftly be posted to England on the money he made. He sold two. Both to Jamaicans who tearfully remembered the places in the pictures from their youth. The money he made clinked in his pocket. But he was not downcast. He had another plan, he said.

It was while he was placing an advertisement in the *Daily Gleaner* for his services – as a storeman or a driver or a clerk or a watchman or a dairyman or a messenger – under the ex-servicemen's section headed 'Help Those Who Helped', that he saw the notice about a ship that was leaving for England. The *Empire Windrush,* sailing on 28 May. The cost of the passage on this retired troop-ship was only twenty-eight pounds and ten shillings.

'Of course, this is twenty-eight pounds and ten shillings I have not got,' he said.

And at that moment – as Gilbert became demoralized for the first time in the face of his impossible endeavour – I had cause to thank Mr Philip and Miss Ma for a lesson they had long taught me. Prudence. A small amount of my wage every week I placed into the building society for a rainy day. And the days before Gilbert left were the rainiest the island had ever seen. 'I can lend you the money,' I told him.

Dumbstruck, he gaped like an idiot before a smile turned one corner of his mouth. 'Your mother never tell you, neither a lender nor a borrower be?'

'You can pay me back.'

'Oh, I know that, Miss Mucky Foot[2]. But what I don't know is why you lend me the money.'

'So you can go to England.' Again he was silent, so I carried on: 'I will lend you the money, we will be married and you can send for me to come to England when you have a place for me to live.'

'Oh, woe!' he shouted. 'Just say that again because I think me ears playing a trick on me there.'

'You can send for me when you are settled.'

'Not that bit. I know that bit. I hear that bit. It was the bit about a marriage.'

'How else will I come? A single woman cannot travel on her own – it would not look good. But a married woman might go anywhere she pleased.'

It took Gilbert only two hours to decide to ask me if I would marry him. And he shook my hand when I said yes, like a business deal had been struck between us.

In the breath it took to exhale that one little word, England became my destiny. A dining table in a dining room set with four chairs. A starched tablecloth embroidered with bows. Armchairs in the sitting room places around a small wood fire. The house is modest – nothing fancy, no show – the kitchen small but with everything I need to prepare meals. We eat rice and peas on Sunday with chicken and corn, but in my English kitchen roast meat with two vegetables and even fish and chips bubble on the stove. My husband fixes the window that sticks and the creaky board on the veranda. I sip hot tea by an open window and look on my neighbours in the adjacent and opposite dwelling. I walk to the shop where I am greeted with manners, 'Good day', politeness, 'A fine day today', and refinement, 'I trust you are well?' A red bus, a cold morning and daffodils blooming with all the colours of the rainbow.

Gilbert cut a surprisingly smart figure at the wedding. We were both astonished to see the other looking so elegant. Gilbert, taking my hand in front of the altar, whispered softly, 'You look nice.'

Excerpt from "Small Island" by Andrea Levy, Headline Publ., 2004

1 Mrs Anderson: the narrator's landlady

2 Miss Mucky Foot: Gilbert refers to the narrator as "Miss Mucky Foot" because the first time they met she fell and got dirty.

**Worksheet: Levy, "Small Island"**

maximum number of points attainable

## I. Questions on the text

Read all the questions first, then answer them in the given order. Use your own words as far as is appropriate.

1. Explain why Gilbert and the narrator get married. — 10
2. What do Gilbert's business projects and his experiences reveal about his character? — 20
3. How does the narrator's use of language reflect her attitude towards Gilbert's business projects? Refer to three examples. — 10
4. Examine the way in which the narrator's character determines the development of the relationship between her and Gilbert. — 20
5. What does England represent for the two protagonists? — 20
6. Analyse the time structure and the use of tenses and show how they are related to the narrative perspective. — 20

## II. Composition

Choose *one* of the following topics. Write about 250 to 300 words. — 50

1. Setting up your own business is the best professional choice you can make. Discuss.
2. To embrace the new you have to leave the old behind. Discuss.
3. Marriage. Show how this theme is dealt with in a literary work by an English-speaking writer.
4. Fifty years after the arrival of the *Empire Windrush* in Britain the former passenger Gilbert Joseph is being interviewed on his life as an immigrant. Write up the historian's interview with him.

## III. Translation

Translate the following text into German: — 50

200

Dr Strand's report[1] is a timely reminder to government and schools of what black Caribbean parents have been protesting about for years. His research-based evidence has been preceded by the findings of black *supplementary schools*[2] and the experience of frustrated parents up and down the land for decades, which is that teachers' low expectations and stereotypical beliefs regarding the ability of black Caribbean children and the quality of teaching that flows from them, are leading to educational underachievement, low student aspirations and an alienation from learning that encourages poor behaviour and discipline and low self-worth.

Forty years ago, the very first parliamentary report on race relations charged that West Indian parents had overly high aspirations for their children and a tendency to equate length of time spent in school with the quality of school outcomes. Little has changed since. Indeed, now that three generations of Caribbean heritage people have been through the British schooling system, teachers' professional socialization with regard to teaching black Caribbean children has been largely influenced by expectations about challenging behaviour, low aspirations and underachievement. Hardly surprising, therefore, that less than 50 % of newly qualified teachers feel they have the competence and cultural awareness to deal with black students, especially in urban settings.

From: *The Guardian,* John Gus, September 5, 2008

Annotations

1 Dr Strand: a psychologist who published a report on schools' institutional racism on September 5th 2008

2 supplementary schools: not to be translated (schools which provide a range of educational opportunities outside usual school hours either related to cultural or religious issues, or the home languages of a particular community)

## Lösungsvorschlag

### I. Questions on the text

1. As for Gilbert, his motivation for getting married is very clear: he wants to go to England, which he knows from the war and where he thinks he will find a better life ("opportunity opened in England as abundant as fruit on Jamaican trees", ll. 13/14). But unfortunately he has not got the money, not even for an obviously comparatively cheap voyage on a ship that will be sailing for England in the near future.
   The narrator also wants to go to England, but her reasons are not so clearly defined in the text. When she learns of Gilbert's situation, she offers to help him by lending him the money she has been saving over the years. In return, she asks him to marry her and then send for her to come and join him as his lawfully wedded wife, since she feels she cannot travel to England as an unmarried woman. Thus, their marriage is "like a business deal" (l. 64) rather than a romantic occasion.

2. Gilbert's mind is firmly fixed on settling down in England. In order to achieve this aim, he tries to make money by setting up some business. His first endeavour is undertaken with a cousin of his: keeping bees and then selling honey seems to be "foolproof" (l. 25), but it soon turns out to be a failure and he loses all the money he has invested. Next, he tries to start a business on his own, selling postcards to tourists this time. This "money-making idea" (l. 31) fails too. Then he wants to offer his services by putting an advertisement in a Jamaican newspaper saying that he will be willing to take just about any job, be it "a storeman or a driver or a clerk …" (ll. 38/39).
   The narrator characterizes Gilbert's wish of "returning to England" as "more than an ambition" (l. 11): she calls it his "mission, a calling, even a duty" (ll. 11/12). So he seems persistent, almost stubborn in the pursuit of his dream. Even his failures neither "deter" him nor "cast him down" (ll. 31/36); he remains optimistic and inventive when it comes to finding new ideas to raise money.
   Gilbert seems rather naïve and blinded by his dream, which is why he rushes into new enterprises without even giving a second thought to whether the project is realistic or not. That is why he trusts his cousin so readily, and that is also why he consents to marry the narrator, even though he hardly knows her. At that moment in his life he is so desperate that he would probably marry anyone who offered him the chance to make his dream come true: "It took Gilbert only two hours to decide to ask me if I would marry him." (l. 63)

3. *The text contains more than just three examples of how the narrator's language reflects her attitude towards Gilbert and his business projects, so you can easily find others than the ones we quote. Before giving these, though, you will have to discuss briefly Hortense's attitude.*

   The narrator is much more pragmatic and realistic in her attitude towards marriage and her future life. She has been sensible enough to save some money "for a rainy day" (l. 47). She does not think very much of Gilbert's business projects; she even dismisses his idea of "honey producing money" as "crazy" (l. 24). She considers Gilbert to be somewhat naïve and easy to handle, which is expressed in the ironic and sometimes even patronizing tone in which she speaks of him. She refers to him losing all his money through the bee business as a "small setback" (l. 31). And when Gilbert wants to make money by selling postcards to tourists who – as he imagined – would come "flocking to this island" (l. 32), she comments dryly on his second failure with the short sentence: "He sold two." (l. 34)

4. *Here again, you have to find out the important features of the narrator's character before you can answer this task and examine its influence on the relationship between her and Gilbert.*

   When characterizing herself, the narrator uses "prudence" (l. 46) as a keyword. She saved "a small amount of [her] wage every week … for a rainy day" (ll. 46–47). This money enables her now to come up with her proposal. She also seems to be a very determined and resolute woman because in those days it would normally have been the man's duty to suggest getting married. This is even more surprising when we see that Hortense has quite traditional views, which are shown in her vision of her future life in England (ll. 65–75): it will be she who will do the cooking. A part of being prudent is also the fact that she is calculating: she sees that Gilbert had become "demoralized for the first time" (l. 44) and takes advantage of his desperate situation.

   On the other hand, she is adventurous and takes a risk when she suggests to Gilbert that she will lend him the money for the voyage. She knows that she will be left behind in Jamaica, and she can only hope that Gilbert will send for her to join him in England, even though she knows that he is not good with money. She probably feels that with all his naivety and enthusiasm he is a 'nice guy' and that he will be grateful enough to fulfil his part of the bargain. That trust in him also comes from the fact that she thinks she is slightly superior to her future husband.

   At the end of the story, at the wedding she probably feels sure that she has done the right thing.

5. For both protagonists, England represents something like paradise. Of course, there are slight differences between their backgrounds and their expectations. Gilbert's ideas seem a little more enthusiastic, since he has been there before. Even though he experienced England only during the war as a soldier, he sees it as a land of "opportunity", (ll. 13/14) which obviously means to him finding a job or opening up a business of his own. He also has the feeling that England owes him some kind of reward for his services as a soldier and that he has a right to live there.

   Although the narrator seems to have a brother or some other relative living in England (ll. 16–19), this has left no lasting impression on her. Yet, she calls it her "destiny" (l. 65). The narrator's ideas seem a little more down-to-earth. Her ambitions are to lead a better and more comfortable life than in Jamaica. She wants a "modest" house, "nothing fancy" (ll. 67/68) copying the lifestyle she thinks is that of the English middle-class: "… roast meat with two vegetables and even fish and chips bubble on the stove … I sip hot tea by an open window …" (ll. 69–75).

6. The beginning and the end of this text are like a frame: in the first part (ll. 1–10) the narrator tells her landlady, who is obviously very surprised, about her plan to get married to Gilbert; the final paragraph (ll. 76–78) gives us a glimpse of their wedding. The main section in the middle (ll. 11–64) consists of snippets, in which the narrator tells us about how her relationship with Gilbert began and how they reached their very sudden marriage agreement. All these events are related in the past tense.
   There is, however, one more paragraph (ll. 65–75), where the narrator uses the present tense to describe her vision of their future life in England. This makes her ideas and hopes appear more vivid and real.
   The narrative perspective is that of a first-person narrator who is part of the story and tells us about her own emotions and thoughts. Although the perspective is limited by that because we see everything through her eyes only, we can say that this makes the text more authentic and livelier, as the narrator thus allows us a more direct approach to the events and to her ideas.
   Both the time structure and the use of two different tenses give the narrator the chance to guide the reader through the story in the way she wishes to: she tells us only what she thinks is necessary, and she does so when she feels like it.

## II. Composition

1. With only a few more weeks of school ahead of us, I have had quite a number of discussions and talks with my friends and my parents about our future professions. Of course we discussed not only what we were going to do but also the way we were going to work. Since finding a permanent employment in a company does not seem to be as easy or as common as it was in our parents' generation, the idea of setting up one's own business seems to suggest itself to many people as the best professional choice one can make.
   There are a number of advantages when you are self-employed. You must certainly identify much more with your job and your business, which will give you a lot more satisfaction in the long run. There are many more choices you have to make, and there is also a lot more responsibility. If you want to succeed, you will have to be creative and inventive. All this can make a profession much more exciting and more interesting. The most important advantage of a self-employed career is undoubtedly the fact that you are working basically only for your own interests and your own needs. There is nobody you are dependent upon – except, of course, market forces and changes. Even though that makes life riskier, it will also make it more colourful and will add more variety.
   On the other hand, many people will argue that you have to be made for a life that does not offer the security of being employed. But when you come to think of it, today even big old traditional companies do not really offer that security any longer. We have seen a good many of them come crashing down within the last few years, and I do not think we have reached the end of the economic crisis which has caused all this turmoil.
   To sum up, I believe that our generation will have to be more flexible when it comes to the choice of our jobs. And that includes considering a self-employed career as well – even if you think you may not be the right person for that.

2. One of my favourite subjects at school has been history. What I like about it is not only that you learn a lot about the origins of our society today, but that history also teaches you that things have been changing constantly and will probably go on doing so forever and ever.
   If one takes into account only the comparatively short period of the last 5,000 years of Old World history, one can only be amazed at the huge changes that mankind has gone through. Even though this process was certainly filled with a lot of pain and suffering,

even though whole peoples and civilizations were swept away, I firmly believe that in the end the human race has benefited enormously: many things that were bad were replaced by something good, and what was good was very often replaced by something even better. One only has to look at the technological and scientific progress man has made. However much one may admire the pyramids of the ancient Egyptians or the Great Wall of China, we have come a long way since then, and I can personally say that I am very happy to be living in today's world. These examples show that you do not necessarily need to leave the old behind to embrace the new. We can always learn from the past and use the achievements of the past as a basis to refine and improve.
What is true on the grand scale of human history can also be said on the smaller scale of one's personal biography. I am at a point in my life when a great change is taking place: the transition from school to what everybody calls 'real life'. I am deeply looking forward to this new stage in my life. I would, however, not be able to cope with the challenges of this new stage if I had not acquired a certain degree of wisdom and a number of skills in the past few years. I am sure that I will neither regret leaving school nor will I look back on it in anger. I am just glad I can start something new, which I hope will give me more independence, better opportunities and a wider range of chances to try out my abilities. This leads me back to the main question of whether to embrace the new you have to leave the old behind. A certain open-mindedness is of course necessary, but I am convinced that we will only be able to face the future if we do not forget about the past.

3. *Innumerable literary works deal with the subject of love. When it comes to heroine and hero finally getting married, however, most authors close the last page. Marriage does not seem to be a topic that interests the reading audiences too much. The case becomes even more desperate when we look at the books read at school. The choice is not overwhelming: Shakespeare's* The Taming of the Shrew, *some novels by Jane Austen, Ian McEwan's* On Chesil Beach ... *In the case of an emergency like this, we found that Nick Hornby's* About A Boy *can offer a good example..*

Nick Hornby's novel *About a Boy* is in fact about two boys: one of them is Marcus, a twelve-year-old, struggling with his status as an outsider. The other 'boy' is Will Freeman, who in spite of his 36 years is not really grown up: he is not interested in a professional career, nor does he show any inclination to get married and start a family. Which brings us to our topic, how the theme of marriage is dealt with in this book.
*About a Boy* is full of singles looking for a partner. Marcus' mother is separated from his father, who lives with a new partner in Cambridge. Will has had a number of affairs, which he usually ended when things were getting too serious for him. Now he is looking for someone new, so he joins a group of single parents hoping to find a new partner. As it turns out, all the other members of this group are women. Ellie, the girl from Marcus' school who takes an interest in him, also lives alone with her mother, who in turn has casual affairs. Rachel, the woman Will meets at the end of the story, has a son whose father is living in the USA at the moment. Their only contact is by telephone. Even though Rachel and Will begin a relationship, the reader has the feeling that this will not necessarily lead to marriage and family life.
All of the adults have experienced living together with someone else at least once in their lifetime, but none of them have succeeded. What we get in the novel are dysfunctional families and single people trying to build a relationship. It is obvious that there is still the idea that people get more out of life when living with a partner. But it seems that this does not work any more. Which makes this book, which seems to be so funny when first reading it, rather sad on second thoughts.

4. *"Fifty years after the arrival" of Gilbert Joseph in England – that makes him a man in his seventies in the year 1998. Besides that, he may now speak proper English instead of the Caribbean Creole he uses in the text – which is good for you, since no one can expect you to be able to write that language. On the other hand, it is a good topic, so our writer got a bit carried away and wrote more than 300 words. If you want to come closer to that figure, we suggest a few cuts which are marked by brackets (), although that may make the text less colourful..*

Historian (= H): Mr Joseph, you arrived in England 50 years ago. What was the beginning of your life on this island like?
Gilbert Joseph (= GJ): Actually, England was more of a dream to me then, so I had no real idea of what I was going to do. (Besides, there were not many black people from Jamaica living in London in those days.) However, I had been given the address of a man from Kingston who (had stayed in London after the war. He) had opened a small restaurant and owned a flat where he rented out rooms to fellow Jamaicans.
H: Was it difficult to find work?
GJ: Well, I was given some odd chores in the restaurant like washing the dishes or cleaning the floors, which paid for the rent and food. But I wanted to save up a little money to be able to pay for my wife's passage. (You see, she had stayed behind and I had promised to send for her as soon as possible.) So I had to look for other jobs.
H: So what did you do then?
GJ: Well, I accompanied my employer very often to the central market where he bought vegetables and fish and meat for his restaurant. I started an extra job at a fruit dealer's, helping to unload and stack up bananas and oranges and so on. One day I (had this idea and I) said to him: Why don't we put up a small stall selling good strong coffee and sandwiches to the people who might like something in the early morning hours to keep them going?
H: And that proved an instant success?
GJ: Oh yes, there had been no such thing before. People came flocking by (to have a quick cup of good hot strong Jamaican coffee. It was the espresso of those days!). And within a few months I had made so much money that I could send for Hortense to join me.
H: And that was the beginning of 'Uncle Joseph's Coffee Corner'?
GJ: Well, yes. Actually, it was my wife's idea. (Although I must say she prefers a cup of good English tea with a biscuit. She has always been an enterprising woman anyway). When she arrived, she saw the possibilities of opening another stall in the City. Well, all these business people enjoyed having their cup of coffee in the afternoon, too.
H: And the next Coffee Corners were opened soon after, weren't they?
GJ: Well, not so quickly, but every second year we opened another one. And in between we had our three children, one every second year, too. They are running the business now. And we're still doing very well. People like our brew! And the Caribbean atmosphere!
H: Thank you for this interview, Mr Joseph! (And good luck for the future!)

## III. Translation

Dr. Strands Bericht erinnert Regierung und Schulen zur rechten Zeit daran, worüber schwarze Eltern aus der Karibik[1]seit Jahren Klage führen. Seine auf wissenschaftlicher Forschung gegründeten Beweise sind jahrzehntelang von den Erkenntnisse schwarzer *supplementary schools* und den Erfahrungen frustrierter Eltern im ganzen Lande vorweggenommen worden[2], dass nämlich die niedrige Erwartungshaltung und die stereotypen[3] Vorstellungen der Lehrer hinsichtlich der Fähigkeiten schwarzer Kinder aus der Karibik und die Qualität des Lehrens, die sich daraus ergibt[4], dazu führen, dass in der Schule weniger geleistet wird als möglich wäre, dass Schüler geringeren Ehrgeiz haben und sich dem Lernen entfremden, was wiederherum[5] schlechtes Benehmen, mangelnde Disziplin und niedriges Selbstwertgefühl unterstützt[6].

Vor vierzig Jahren beklagte der allererste Parlamentsbericht über die Beziehungen der Rassen, dass Eltern von den Westindischen Inseln allzu hohe Ambitionen für ihre Kinder hätten und dazu neigten, die Länge der Zeit, die in der Schule verbracht wurde, mit der Qualität der Schulergebnisse gleichzusetzen. Seitdem hat sich (nur) wenig geändert. In der Tat, jetzt da drei Generationen von Menschen mit karibischer Herkunft[7] das britische Schulsystem durchlaufen haben, wird die berufliche Sozialisation von Lehrern, was das Unterrichten von schwarzen Kindern aus der Karibik angeht, immer noch weitgehend beeinflusst davon, dass sie schwieriges[8] Benehmen, geringen Ehrgeiz und unzulängliche Leistungen erwarten. Es überrascht deshalb kaum, dass weniger als die Hälfte der neu ausgebildeten Lehrer glauben, dass sie die Fähigkeit und das kulturelle Bewusstsein[9] haben, mit schwarzen Schülern umzugehen, vor allem gerade im städtischen Umfeld.

Anmerkungen

1 black Caribbean: diese Kombination in Analogie zu afro-amerikanisch auch als afro-karibisch übersetzbar

2 freier: Vor seinen auf wissenschaftlicher Forschung gegründeten Beweisen haben jahrzehntelang schwarze supplementary schools herausgefunden und frustrierte Eltern im ganzen Land die Erfahrung gemacht, dass nämlich …

3 *auch:* klischeehaften

4 *auch:* resultiert

5 stilistische Ergänzung

6 „fördern, ermutigen" wirken im Deutschen in diesem Zusammenhang zu positiv

7 *auch:* Hintergrund

8 *auch:* problematisch; provozierend

9 *auch:* Einfühlungsvermögen, Verständnis

# Ihre Meinung ist uns wichtig!

Ihre Anregungen sind uns immer willkommen. Bitte informieren Sie uns mit diesem Schein über Ihre Verbesserungsvorschläge!

| Titel-Nr. | Seite | Vorschlag |
|---|---|---|
| | | |
| | | |
| | | |
| | | |
| | | |
| | | |
| | | |
| | | |
| | | |

Bitte hier abtrennen

Bitte hier abtrennen

**Zutreffendes bitte ankreuzen!**

**Die Absenderin/der Absender ist:**

- ☐ Lehrer/in in den Klassenstufen: ______
- ☐ Fachbetreuer/in
  Fächer: ______
- ☐ Seminarlehrer/in
  Fächer: ______
- ☐ Regierungsfachberater/in
  Fächer: ______
- ☐ Oberstufenbetreuer/in
- ☐ Schulleiter/in
- ☐ Referendar/in, Termin 2. Staatsexamen: ______
- ☐ Leiter/in Lehrerbibliothek
- ☐ Leiter/in Schülerbibliothek
- ☐ Sekretariat
- ☐ Eltern
- ☐ Schüler/in, Klasse: ______
- ☐ Sonstiges: ______

**Unterrichtsfächer:** (Bei Lehrkräften!)

______

19-VD9

Bitte ausfüllen und im frankierten Umschlag an uns einsenden. Für Fensterkuverts geeignet.

STARK Verlag
Postfach 1852
85318 Freising

**Kennen Sie Ihre Kundennummer?**
**Bitte hier eintragen.**

**Absender** (Bitte in Druckbuchstaben!)

Name/Vorname

Straße/Nr.

PLZ/Ort/Ortsteil

Telefon privat

Geburtsjahr

E-Mail

**Schule/Schulstempel** (Bitte immer angeben!)

*(Bitte blättern Sie um)*